Ephrem the Syrian's Hymns on the Unleavened Bread

Texts from Christian Late Antiquity

30

Series Editor

George Anton Kiraz

TeCLA (Texts from Christian Late Antiquity) is a series presenting ancient Christian texts both in their original languages and with accompanying contemporary English translations.

Ephrem the Syrian's Hymns on the Unleavened Bread

Translation and Introduction by

J. Edward Walters

gorgias press
2012

Gorgias Press LLC, 954 River Road, Piscataway, NJ, 08854, USA

www.gorgiaspress.com

Copyright © 2012 by Gorgias Press LLC

All rights reserved under International and Pan-American Copyright Conventions. No part of this publication may be reproduced, stored in a retrieval system or transmitted in any form or by any means, electronic, mechanical, photocopying, recording, scanning or otherwise without the prior written permission of Gorgias Press LLC.

2012 ܓ

ISBN 978-1-4632-0159-3   **ISSN 1935-6846**

Printed in the United States of America

To Kathleen McVey

Table of Contents

Table of Contents vii
Preface ix
Acknowledgements xi
List of Abbreviations xiii
Introduction 1
Text and Translation 11
Index of Biblical References 101

Preface

This translation began as an assignment for Dr. Kathleen McVey's Ph.D. seminar on Ephrem the Syrian in the spring of 2011. At the outset of the course, I had no intention of translating a selection of Ephrem's works, let alone publishing a translation. The first week of class, each student was assigned to lead the discussion for one week of the seminar, and my week just so happened to be on Ephrem's *Paschal Hymns*. I knew immediately that I had been assigned one of the only sets of hymns we covered in the seminar that did not yet exist in a full English translation, so I began working on a rough translation that I could use for my presentation in class. I knew, of course, of the German and French translations, but in order to really grasp the material, I wanted to make a translation of my own.

As I was translating, I realized how intriguing these hymns were, and I wanted to dive even further into the depths of <u>Ephrem's poetic comparison of the Jewish and Christian practices of Passover</u>. So, in consultation with Dr. McVey, I decided that my seminar paper for the semester would be a translation of Ephrem's "Hymns on the Unleavened Bread" accompanied by a brief study of its contents and main features. The present publication, albeit revised significantly, is the end result of that project.

James Edward Walters
Novermber 30, 2011
First Day of Advent

Acknowledgements

First of all, I would like to thank Dr. Kathleen McVey for allowing me to take on this project as a seminar paper in her course. I would also like to thank my classmates in the course: Emilee Walker Cornetta, Philip Michael Forness, Alex Kocar, Kate McCray, Courtney Palmbush, and Inseo Song, all of whom provided helpful feedback on the readability of my translation. Special thanks is due to Philip Michael Forness, who, in addition to reading the translation in the course, also read and provided feedback on a revised version of the edited text and translation well after the seminar was over.

Thanks is also due to George A. Kiraz, who graciously agreed to accept this work for publication and to all the employees of Gorgias Press who helped in the process of typing, editing, and type-setting the text. I would also like to thank Fr. Elie Joseph Bali, who added the West Syriac vocalization to the previously unvocalized text. Any mistakes are the fault of the author and not those who proofread or helped edit the text.

I hope that this volume will be of service to all who are interested in Syriac studies, the study of Ephrem, Jewish-Christian relations, and even more broadly, the religious literature of late antiquity. Syriac sources like Ephrem have largely been ignored in the study of late antique Christianity, primarily because of linguistic barriers. I hope that this small contribution will aid in spreading knowledge of Ephrem and early Syriac Christianity to a broader audience.

LIST OF ABBREVIATIONS

CSCO	Corpus Scriptorum Christianorum Orientalium
H.Azym.	Hymn on the Unleavened Bread
H.Cruc.	Hymn on the Crucifixion
H.Res.	Hymn on the Resurrection
SC	Sources Chrétiennes

INTRODUCTION

Ephrem the Syrian (d. 373 CE), long acknowledged as the chief representative of early Syriac literature and the Syriac expression of Christianity along the Roman/Persian border, still remains a distant figure in the broader history of early Christianity. While many of Ephrem's works have been made available in critical editions and modern translations,[1] Ephrem's entire corpus is yet to be translated into English. While most scholars are able to read Ephrem in German or French translations, the works of Ephrem need to be made more available to a broader readership so that early Syriac Christianity can attain its proper standing within the larger early Christian world.

The subject of the present project is the set of writings known as the "Hymns on the Unleavened Bread," which is part of a larger collection of Ephrem's hymns known as the Paschal Hymns.[2] These hymns have already been translated into German,[3] Italian,[4] and French,[5] and while a few of the

---

[1] Scholars who work with Ephrem are particularly indebted to Edmund Beck, who edited and translated most of the authentic works of Ephrem. Through his efforts, Beck produced over thirty volumes in the CSCO series dedicated solely to Ephrem's writings.

[2] In addition to the Hymns on the Unleavened Bread, the Paschal Hymns collection also includes "Hymns on the Crucifixion" and "Hymns on the Resurrection."

[3] E. Beck, *Des Heiligen Ephraem des Syrers Paschahymnen: (De azymis, De Crucifixione, De Resurrectione)*, CSCO 248-249 (Louvain: Secrétariat du CorpusSCO, 1964).

[4] I. de Francesco, *Efrem il Siro, Inni Pasquali sugli azzimi, sulla crocifissione, sulla risurrezione, introduzione, traduzione e note* (Milan, 2001).

[5] G.A.M. Rouwhorst, *Les Hymnes Pascales d'Éphrem de Nisibe, II: Textes*, Supplements to Vigiliae Christianae 7,2 (Leiden: Brill, 1989); D. Cerbelaud, *Éphrem. Célébrons la Pâque: Hymnes sur les Azymes, sur la Crucifixion, sur la Résurrection*, Le Pères dans la foi 58 (Paris, 1995); François Cassingena-Trévedy, *Éphrem de Nisibe: Hymnes Pascales*, SC 502 (Paris: Cerf, 2006).

hymns have been translated into English,[6] there is no complete English translation of the Paschal Hymns in publication. And while there is a small body of literature on the Paschal Hymns, this collection of Ephrem's writings has not been fully explored by modern scholarship.[7]

THE TEXT

The Hymns on the Unleavened Bread collection is comprised of twenty-one hymns.[8] However, it appears that there are actually two sets of hymns in this collection: Hymns 1-2 and Hymns 3-21 appear to represent distinct units. While the content and themes of *H.Azym.* 1-2 generally corresponds to *H.Azym.* 3-21,[9] the first two hymns of the Unleavened Bread collection stand apart from the rest of the collection in three ways: 1) they are set to a different melody,[10] 2) they have a different structure in both lines per strophe and syllables per line,[11] and 3) they are organized as an acrostic, whereas the rest of the Unleavened Bread collection does not utilize this literary feature.[12]

---

[6] Unleavened Bread Hymn 3 is found in Brock, "The Poetic Artistry of St. Ephrem: An Analysis of H. Azym. III," *Parole de l'Orient* 6-7 (1975-76): 24-25; Resurrection hymns 1-2 are found in idem., *The Harp of the Spirit. Eighteen Poems of Saint Ephrem* (London, 1984), 27-30, 73-76; and Unleavened Bread Hymn 19 is found in Christine Shepardson, *Anti-Judaism and Christian Orthodoxy: Ephrem's Hymns in Fourth-Century Syria* (Washington, D.C.: CUA Press, 2008), 32-33.

[7] Beyond the translations, which include rather brief introductory materials, French scholar Jean Gribomont has published a series of three articles: "Les hymnes de saint Ephrem sur la Pâque," *Melto* 1-2 (1967): 147-182; "Le triomphe de Pâques d'après saint Ephrem," *Parole de l'Orient* 4 (1973):147-189; and "La tradition liturgique des hymnes pascales de saint Ephrem," *Parole de l'Orient* 4 (1973): 191-244; for a more recent study which is also the most extensive published yet, see Rouwhorst, *Les Hymnes Pascales D'Ephrem de Nisibe, I: Etude, Supplements to Vigiliae Christianae, 7,1* (Leiden, Brill: 1989).

[8] Hymns 8-11, however, are not extant in the primary manuscript for these hymns, and exist only partially in another manuscript.

[9] That is, Hymns 1-2 employ themes that are also prominent within Hymns 3-21, such as "lamb" and sacrificial imagery (*H.Azym.* 1.19; 2.2-6), eucharistic language (*H.Azym.* 2.7), and anti-Jewish polemic (*H.Azym.* 1.11-19).

[10] The melody of *H.Azym.*1-2 is listed as: "The one who is patient in spirit."

[11] Each strophe is three lines with a 5 + 5 meter in each line, Beck, *Paschalhymnen* (Version), iii.

[12] The first hymn goes from ܐ to ܟ and the second goes from ܠ to ܬ. The fact that these hymns form an acrostic and yet do not complete the alphabet begs the

Hymns 3-21 of the Unleavened Bread collection, on the other hand, can be considered a coherent unit likely composed as one continuous work for the following reasons: 1) these hymns are set to the same melody,[13] they display the same meter and structure,[14] and they contain similar content expressed with common literary features. The primary literary feature of these hymns is a comparison of the "paschal lamb" of the Jewish practice of Passover with the "true lamb."[15] This comparison extends throughout the remaining hymns and is expressed in various ways in order to contrast the Jewish Passover with the Christian Passover.

The Syriac text used in this edition is taken from Beck's critical edition, though it is presented in a vocalized Serto script rather than un-vocalized Estrangelo. Textual variants and other critical notes on the Syriac text are not included, as this edition is intended to be a reader-friendly volume.

UNIQUE FEATURES OF THESE HYMNS

Typological Comparison of the Jewish Passover and the Christian Pascha

From the very beginning of the Hymns on the Unleavened Bread, Ephrem makes it clear that typological comparisons will be a major theme.[16] Following this introduction, Ephrem immediately launches into a typological discussion of the exodus, which provides a convenient source of types and symbols for Ephrem on the topic of the Pascha because of the relationship of the exodus to the installation of the Jewish Passover. As is typical for his typological exegesis, Ephrem teases out the exodus

---

question of whether there was a third hymn (or more) to the same melody that would complete the acrostic. Indeed, the first Hymn on the Resurrection in the Paschal Hymns collection is also an incomplete acrostic in which most of the strophes begin with the letter ܩ, despite the fact that none of the other Resurrection Hymns are acrostics.

[13] The heading for *H.Azym.* 3 informs us that the tune is "Gather together to celebrate in the month of Nisan," and the headings for all the remaining hymns say "to the same tune."

[14] Each strophe is two lines with a 5 + 4 meter in each line, Beck, *Paschalhymnen* (Version), iii; Gribomont, "Les hymnes sur la Pâque," 156.

[15] That this is one of the major themes of these hymns is signaled from the very beginning of Hymn 3: "Let us compare both lambs, my brothers, [and] let us see whether they are the same or different / Let us weigh and compare their glories, [those] of the symbolic lamb and of the true lamb" (*H.Azym.* 3.2-3).

[16] *H.Azym.* 3.1-2.

comparison in several ways: Egypt itself serves as a dual type for error and Sheol[17] because the exodus from Egypt is a type for the Christian exodus from error and Sheol.[18] Moreover, Pharaoh also serves as a dual type, representing Death and Satan, because he released the people that he had previously held captive.[19]

Ephrem also argues that the types and symbols of Christ are revealed in Scripture and in nature. For example, in *H.Azym.* 4, Ephrem asserts: "Even the [Jewish] teachers were ashamed that they alienated the Son / for behold, they erred the Law and all its imprints / The prophets bore [his symbols] as servants / [as] examples of the Messiah who rules over all / Nature and Scripture bore together / symbols of the Messiah who rules over all."[20] Throughout the Paschal Hymns, symbols, examples and types are very important for Ephrem, but not only as a flat exegetical tool by which Ephrem explains what things mean. Rather, Ephrem uses typological exegesis in service of the larger rhetorical aim of emptying the Jewish Passover of all its significance in order to present the Christian Pascha as the only true celebration taking place in the month of Nisan.[21]

Not surprisingly for a set of hymns that compares the Jewish Passover with the Christian Pascha, metaphors, imagery, and types involving lambs are prominent, especially among the Hymns on the Unleavened Bread. Ephrem frequently sets up comparisons between Jewish and Christian depictions of lambs by paralleling construct phrases based on the Syriac word for lamb. The Jewish lamb is almost always referred to as the "paschal lamb,"[22] while the Christian lamb is most frequently called the "true lamb" or the "living lamb." The comparison of the lambs, along with Ephrem's rhetorical goal in using this feature, is seen most clearly in *H.Azym.* 6.9-14:

> The lamb of God ate a lamb;
>   who has seen a lamb eat another lamb?
> The true lamb ate the paschal lamb;

---

[17] *H.Azym.* 3.7-9.

[18] The former is a reference to turning away from non-orthodox teaching, and the latter is a reference to the "harrowing" of Hell; for a thorough analysis of Christ's "descent to Sheol" in Ephrem's thought, see Thomas Buchan, "Blessed is He who has brought Adam from Sheol": Christ's descent to the dead in the theology of Saint Ephrem the Syrian (Piscataway, NJ: Gorgias Press, 2004).

[19] *H.Azym.* 3.13-16.

[20] *H.Azym.* 4.22-24.

[21] For an example of this "replacement" typology, see *H.Azym.* 12.1-4.

[22] Though a few others occur: "perishable lamb" and "symbolic lamb."

> the symbol hastened to enter the belly of truth.
> For all the types in the holy of holies
> > dwelt and anticipated the one who fulfills all.
> And when the symbols saw the true lamb,
> > they tore the curtain and stepped out to meet him.
> They were all entirely based on, and established for, him;
> > for they all proclaimed everything [about him] everywhere.
> For in him, the symbols and types were fulfilled,
> > just as he confirmed: "Behold, everything is finished!"

This description is remarkable, not only because of the imagery of cannibal lambs, but also because it succinctly summarizes the way that Ephrem views the Jewish practice of Passover: it only held meaning because it contained symbols, and the ritual lost its meaning when the "true lamb" came and "perfected" all of the symbols. This concept is made even more explicit in the following hymn: "In this feast our Lord dismissed the symbols / that struggled in his proclamation. / In this feast the lamb of truth abolished / the paschal lamb, which had run its course."[23]

Thus, the imagery of the two lambs represents a microcosm of Ephrem's comparison between the Jewish and Christian ritual practice of the Passover: the former was indeed meaningful and served its God-given purpose, but it was only a shadow of things to come. The "true lamb" fulfilled all of the symbols infused within the Passover, rendering both the "paschal lamb" and the broader ritual devoid of meaning. This language begs the question of Ephrem's knowledge of the Jewish Passover in his own community and the element of "competition" that may have existed between the two communities.

The 'People' and the 'Peoples' - The Depiction of the Jews

Ephrem's primary method of distinguishing between Jews and Christians within the Hymns on the Unleavened Bread is the language of "the people" [Jews] and "the peoples" [Christians].[24] Although Ephrem uses these terms rather consistently, some nuance is required to understand the precise referent in some cases. For example, Ephrem uses the phrase "the people"

---

[23] *H.Azym.* 12.3-4.

[24] Occasionally, Ephrem uses "the peoples" in such a way that it is best to translate it as "the Gentiles/the nations," much like the translation of the Greek τὰ ἔθνη; cf. *H.Azym.* 21.9.

[handwritten note:] ※ Ephrem: Fire and the Spirit are in our baptism - Fire and the Spirit are also in the Bread and Cup.

to refer to the Israelites/Jews from any time period. Thus, the Israelites who took part in the first Passover in Egypt, the Jews that rejected Jesus and unwittingly killed him as the "true" paschal lamb, and the Jews of Ephrem's own time are all referred to as "the people" with no apparent distinction. This lack of distinction allows Ephrem to interpret the history of the Jewish people through the lens of Christianity: "the people" in Egypt received a ritual impregnated with symbols of the coming Christ; "the people" in Jesus' time did not understand these symbols, and thus rejected the one for whom they were supposed to be waiting; and "the people" in Ephrem's own time continue to enact a ritual that has been stripped of its meaning because the symbols were fulfilled in Christ.

In this regard, Ephrem typically views the identity of the Jews as frozen in time at the moment when they rejected Jesus. The "people" of Jesus' time is the interpretive lens for both the historical Israelites (cf. *H.Azym.* 17) and the Jews of Ephrem's own day (cf. *H.Azym.* 19). As a result, Ephrem is nearly a perfect candidate for what Miriam Taylor has described as "symbolic anti-Judaism."[25] It is necessary to emphasize the "nearly" of the previous statement however, because, as Christine Shepardson has argued, Ephrem employs a vitriolic anti-Judaic polemic that, although motivated by his enforcement of Nicene orthodoxy, is meant to construct boundaries between Jewish and Christian practices that, presumably, were not enforced prior to Ephrem's appeals to distinguish them.[26] Thus, there is an extent to which Ephrem's anti-Judaism is both "symbolic" and "conflictual,"[27] as Ephrem relies primarily on symbolic, theological ideas to critique concurrent Jews, who are primarily viewed through the lens of the first-century Jews who rejected Jesus, but who nevertheless provide a real community from whom Ephrem feels the need to distinguish and distance

---

[25] More specifically, Ephrem's writings could be considered under the sub-category of "Theological Anti-Judaism," as described in M. Taylor, *Anti-Judaism and Early Christian Identity: A Critique of the Scholarly Consensus* (Leiden: Brill, 1995), 127-169.

[26] As Shepardson says concerning these hymns, using *H.Azym.* 19 as the example par excellence, "In this series of hymns, Ephrem castigates members of his church audience for participating in a festival at the synagogue, and he struggles to draw clear lines between "Jews" and "Christians" and to identify proper "Christian" behavior, such that it coincides with the outcome of the Council of Nicaea," Shepardson, *Anti-Judaism and Christian Orthodoxy*, 31.

[27] See Taylor's discussion of "Conflictual Anti-Judaism" in *Anti-Judaism and Early Christian Identity*, 47-114; see especially the discussion of Melito's "Paschal Homily," 67-74.

his own community.[28] The need to establish boundaries between Jewish and Christian practices is thus the context in which the Hymns on the Unleavened Bread must be read in order to make sense of the anti-Jewish rhetoric.

THE TRANSLATION

Anyone who has attempted to translate Ephrem can appreciate the enormous difficulty of portraying the brilliance of Ephrem's poetic style into any other language.[29] A translation technique that relies upon a rigid, literal approach often renders Ephrem incomprehensible and misses the depth of meaning hiding in elided words. On the other hand, a translation that is too free in rendering Ephrem's words can too easily ignore the word plays that Ephrem frequently employs. As a result, any translator of Ephrem must decide when to emphasize the literal translation and when to provide a more fluid translation, and this method can flux throughout.

In the present translation, I have attempted to strike a balance between the literal and the free translation by representing Ephrem's words and syntax rather literally, yet augmenting this literal translation by providing missing words and phrases and adding additional notes where necessary. The words I have provided are indicated in the translation by brackets [ ]. Any additional notes of explanation, along with references to Scripture, are included in footnotes.

---

[28] A more recent treatment of Ephrem's anti-Judaism (Elena Narinskaya, *Ephrem, a Jewish Sage: A Comparison of the Exegetical Writings of St. Ephrem the Syrian and Jewish Traditions* [Turnhout: Brepols, 2010]) attempts to argue that Ephrem should not be considered a witness of "anti-Judaism" because he so freely adopted exegetical and theological techniques from prior and concurrent Jewish traditions. This thesis, however, begins with a particular definition of anti-Judaism that generally ignores the arguments of Taylor's work on the subject, relies primarily on the "exegetical" works of Ephrem, (i.e. *not* the Paschal Hymns) and ultimately cannot bear the weight of the evidence for anti-Judaism in Ephrem's works that previous scholars (and particularly Shepardson) have established.

[29] As Sebastian Brock states in his introduction to the Hymns on Paradise, "St Ephrem's hymns present the translator with many problems arising out of the condensed and allusive style of his writing," Brock, *St Ephrem the Syrian: Hymns on Paradise* (Crestwood, NY: St. Vladimir's Seminary Press, 1990), 74.

Resources for the Paschal Hymns: Editions, Translations, Studies

Editions

Lamy, T.J. *Sancti Ephraem Syri Hymni et Sermones, 4 Volumes.* Mechliniae, 1882-1902; For "On the Unleavened Bread" and "On the Crucifixion," see Vol. 1 (1882), 567-713; for "On the Resurrection," see Vol. 2 (1886), 742-774.

Beck, E. *Des Heiligen Ephraem des Syrers Paschahymnen.* Corpus Scriptorum Christianorum Orientalium 248, Scriptores syri, 108. Louvain: Secrétariat du CorpusSCO, 1964.

Translations

Beck, E. *Des Heiligen Ephraem des Syrers Paschahymnen.* Corpus Scriptorum Christianorum Orientalium 249, Scriptores syri, 109. Louvain: Secrétariat du CorpusSCO, 1964.

Cassingena-Trévedy, François. *Éphrem de Nisibe: Hymnes Pascales.* Sources Chretien 502. Paris: Cerf, 2006.

Cerbelaud, D. Éphrem, *Célébrons la Pâque: Hymnes sur les Azymes, sur la Crucifixion, sur la Résurrection.* Le Pères dans la foi 58. Paris, 1995.

de Francesco, I. *Efrem il Siro, Inni Pasquali sugli azzimi, sulla crocifissione, sulla risurrezione, introduzione, traduzione e note.* Milan, 2001.

Rouwhorst, G.A.M. *Les Hymnes Pascales d'Éphrem de Nisibe, II: Textes.* Supplements to Vigliliae Christianae 7, 2. Leiden: Brill, 1989.

Studies

Brock, Sebastian P. "The Poetic Artistry of St. Ephrem: An Analysis of H. Azym. III." *Parole de l'Orient* 6-7 (1975-76): 24-25.

Gribomont, Jean. "La tradition liturgique des hymnes pascales de saint Ephrem." *Parole de l'Orient* 4 (1973): 191-244.

_____ "Le triomphe de Pâques d'après saint Ephrem," *Parole de l'Orient* 4 (1973): 147-189.

_____ "Les hymnes de saint Ephrem sur la Pâque." *Melto* 1-2 (1967): 147-182.

Rouwhorst, G.A.M. *Les Hymnes Pascales D'Ephrem de Nisibe, I: Etude.* Supplements to Vigiliae Christianae, 7,1 Leiden: Brill, 1989.

Text and Translation

Hymns on the Unleavened Bread
by the Blessed St. Ephrem

Hymn 1[30]

On the unleavened bread,
to the tune of "The one who is patient in spirit"

1   He who makes all wise came in his love to the foolish,
yet they remained in their foolishness. When he admonished them,
they persecuted, without discernment, the treasure house of discernment.[31]

Response: Praise to the one who sent you!

2   I marvel at your loving mercies, which you have poured out upon the wicked:
for you impoverished your greatness so that you might enrich our poverty,[32]
in order that we, through our hidden treasures, might become friends of those above.

3   He was perfect in his goodness, for he gave reward and taught
the sick one whom he healed. He healed him, and then he taught [him].
The one who learned received a reward, for it was through his healing that he learned.

---

[30] This is an acrostic hymn from ܐ to ܙ.

[31] The word Ephrem uses here, purshana, is a multivalent term with several possible translations. Its meaning ranges from "discernment, judging" to "foreknowledge" and "superior, excellent." It is also a term used for the "host, Eucharistic bread." Based on the language in this strophe concerning wisdom and foolishness, Ephrem likely intends the meaning of "discernment," but the Syriac speaking audience would catch the double entendre.

[32] 2 Cor 8:9

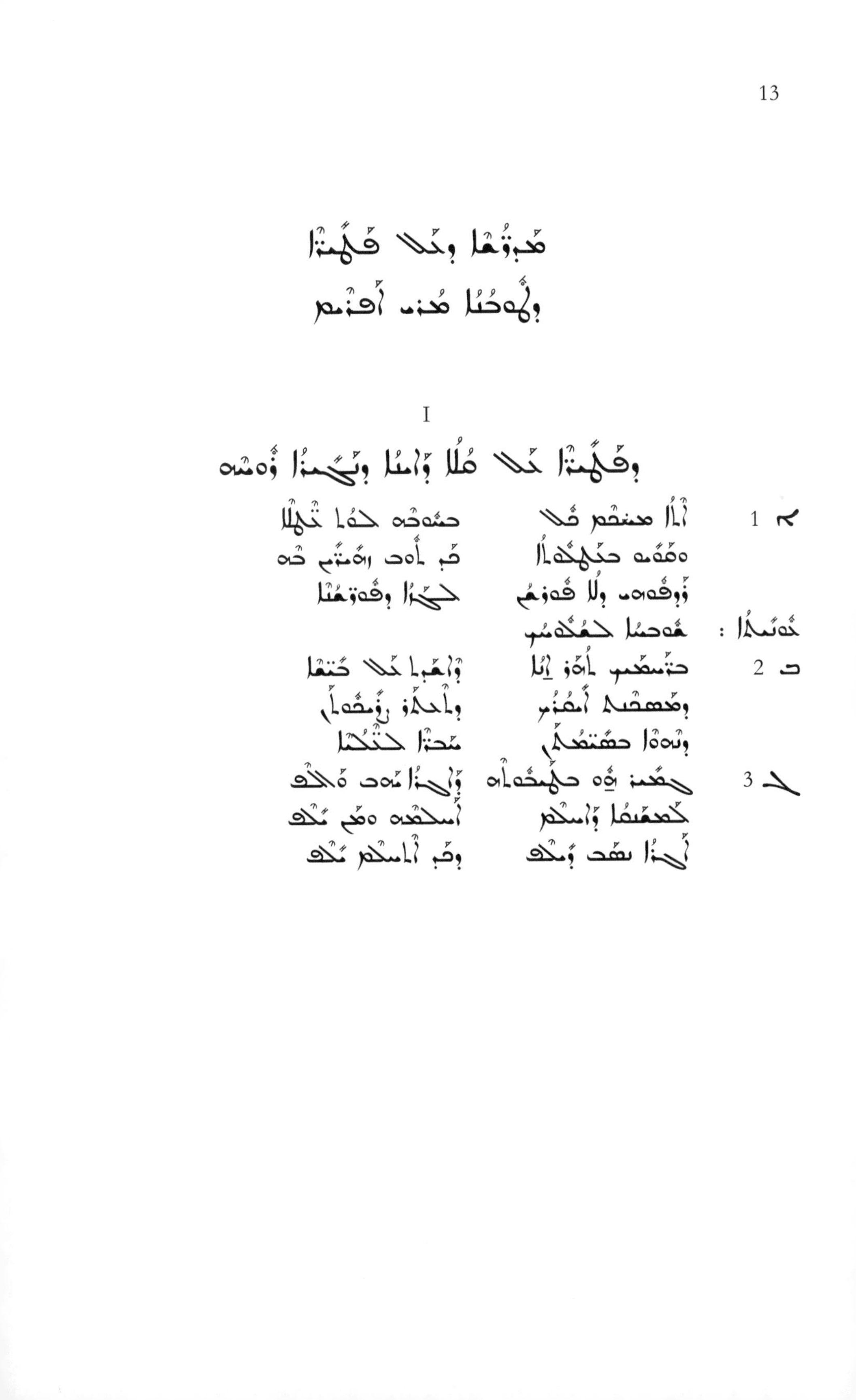

I

א 1

4 He perfected humanity through everything he endured:
while being struck, he kept teaching; while suffering, he continued to make promises.
He was bound like a sheep so that he might keep his promises.

5 The one who judges all judges was judged and interrogated
instead of the one who sinned. For, instead of the wicked,
the just one was interrogated. Praise be to the one who sent him!

6 The good one who came was judged, in his loving mercy, instead of the evil ones.
And this is the amazing thing: they condemned him instead of themselves!
With their own hands, they crucified him instead of their own iniquity.

7 He gave himself for them so that they might live by means of his death.
And like the lamb in Egypt that gave life through the symbol of its master,
he was slain. He gave life, through his love, to the ones who killed him.

8 Because Adam sinned and went astray in Paradise,
the place of pleasures, the just one was beaten instead of him
in the house of judgment, the place of torments.

9 But behold, the good one came in order to perfect the righteous ones
who have carried his symbols. It was through his perfection,
through his completeness, that he perfected his siblings as members [of his body].

10 Even though Adam killed the life within his body,
there was within [his body] a type of the body that has perfected all.
Behold, [through that body] the just are perfected and their sins are pardoned!

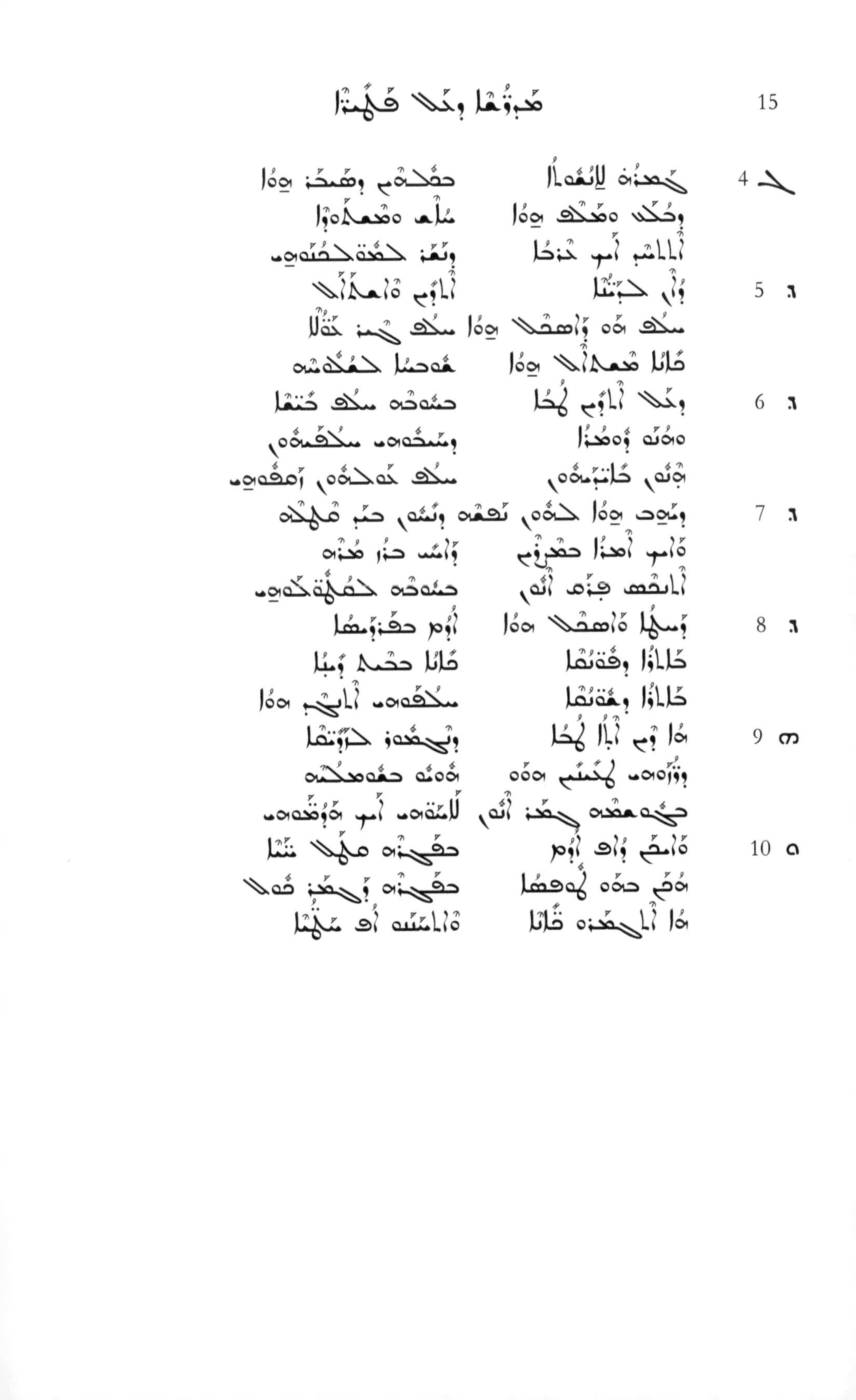

11   The conqueror came down to be defeated, [but] it was not by Satan,
      for he conquered and strangled [Satan]. He was conquered by the
      crucifiers.
      He conquered through his righteousness, and he was conquered by his
      own goodness.

12   He conquered the strong one and he was conquered by the weak
      ones.
      They crucified him because he gave himself. He was conquered in
      order to conquer.
      He conquered his temptations, and he was conquered by his love.

13   He conquered Satan in the desert when [Satan] was provoking him,
      and he was conquered by Satan in a cultivated place when [Satan]
      crucified him.
      While he was being killed, he killed [Satan], so that even in defeat, he
      might conquer [Satan].

14   The wisdom that perfects everything—that speaks with children,
      questions the simple, and disputes with scribes—
      gives intelligence to all [and] sows the truth in all.

15   The wisdom of God[33] came down to the foolish.
      She educated through her teaching and illuminated through her
      interpretation.
      As a reward for her help, they struck her cheeks.

16   The good one, in his goodness, descended to the wicked.
      He repaid that which he did not owe,
      and he was repaid what he had not borrowed.
      They rejected him in two ways: they took from him and repaid him.

17   The good one bore and made others bear: a wonder in both regards!
      For while he made us bear the truth, he took our iniquity from us.
      The needy took his riches, and they burdened him with their sins.

---

[33] 1 Cor 1:21

11		
12		
13		
14		
15		
16		
17		

18 The good one loved the crucifiers through their children,
whom he held and blessed.³⁴ He signified that all of them would become one.
But when he was kissed, they bit him with the mouth of a thief.

19 Behold! The error of that people dwells in hope
and waits for animal sacrifices. It is an evil thing to offer sacrifices again
after he who is the lamb of God [was offered as a sacrifice].

Hymn 2

From the same melody³⁵

1 He is one who knows who he is, [but] he began to hide his knowledge,
and he asked the straying ones: "Whose son is the Messiah?"³⁶
So that his divinity might be made known, he asked about himself.

Response: Blessed is he who was sacrificed for us!

2 The lamb of truth knew that the priests had become defiled,
that the religious leaders³⁷ had become unclean, and that they were not sufficient for him.
He became, for his own body, the priest and high priest.

3 The priests of that people slaughtered the high priest,
for our priest was the sacrifice. Through his sacrifice, he eliminated sacrifices.
On every side, he extended his help.

---

³⁴ Mk 10:16
³⁵ Continues the acrostic of Hymn 1 from ܜ to ܫ.
³⁶ Matt 22:42 Jesus asked the Pharisees
³⁷ Ephrem employs two words, both of which mean priest, so I have attempted to demonstrate this variation.

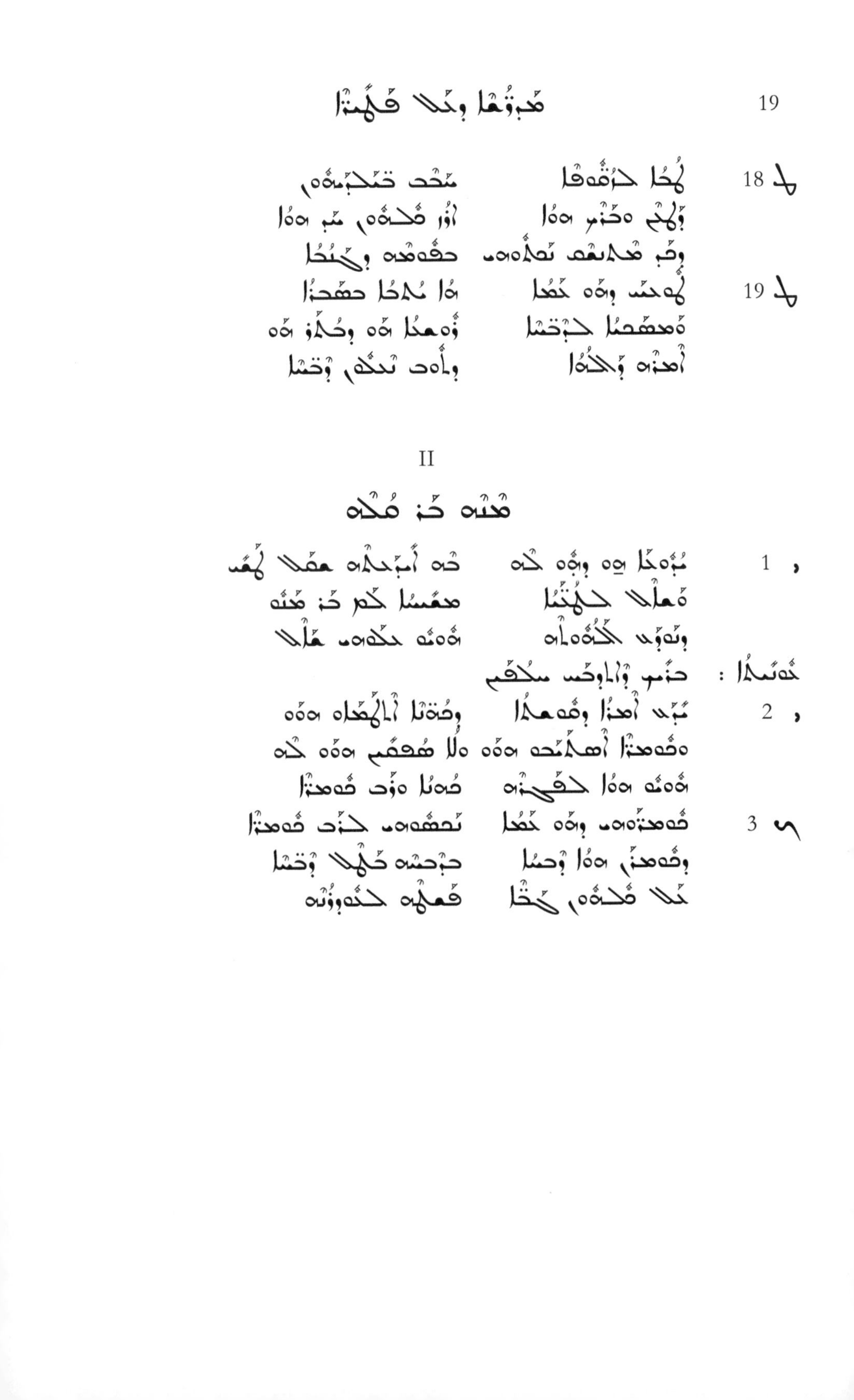

II

4   The priests who were better than the animals
    slaughtered and performed animal sacrifices.
    The priest was made holy by a lamb that was not holy.

5   There is no lamb that will be greater than the lamb of glory.
    Because the priests were earthly and the lamb was heavenly,
    he became for himself both the sacrifice and the sacrificer.

6   For the imperfect priests were not worthy to sacrifice
    the lamb that was without blemish. He became a peace offering,
    and he made peace with the heights and depths through his blood that
    makes peace for all.

7   He broke the bread with his hands as a symbol for the sacrifice of his body.
    He mixed the cup with his hands as a symbol for the sacrifice of his blood.
    He sacrificed and offered himself, the priest of our atonement.

8   He clothed himself in the priesthood of Melchizedek, his type,
    who did not offer sacrifices.[38] He gave the bread and the wine,
    but he dismissed the priesthood [which was] weary from libations.

9   The king from the house of David—his servants blasphemed him.
    Being insane, they declared him insane.[39] By alienating him, they demonstrated
    that they had gone insane, had been deceived, and had blasphemed their king.

10 The kingship of the house of David rushed eagerly to the son of David.
    It saw him and rejoiced. Zion received the good news, [but]
    she saw the beauty that enlightens all and became gloomy.

---

[38] Gen 14:18
[39] Mk 3:21

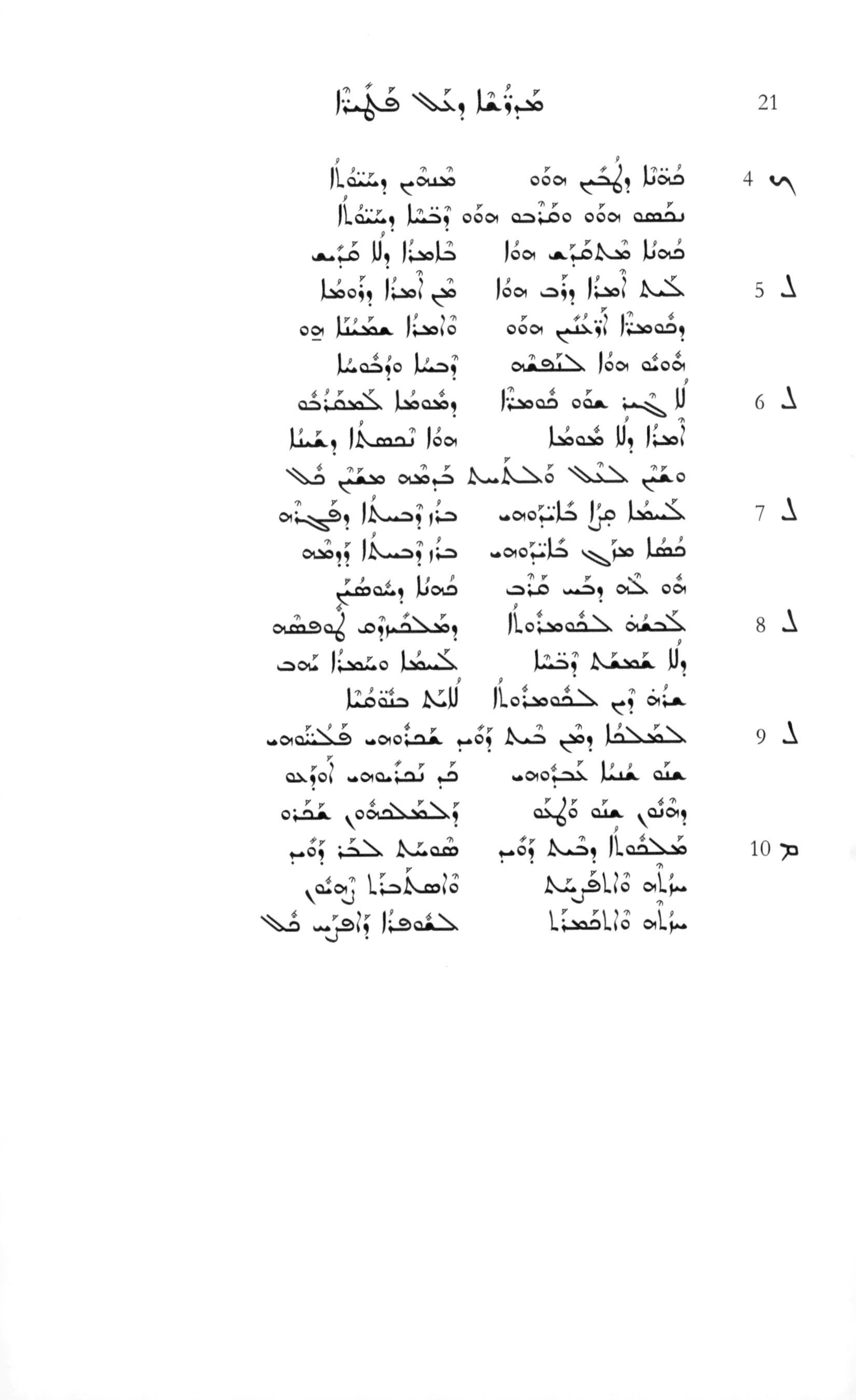

11 The people called him a prophet—he who is the Lord of prophecy.[40]
    Their honor is a reproach, [for] they turned and declared him a madman.[41]
    Their honor is foolishness, and they blasphemed the truth.

12 If he had been [only] a prophet, he would have been equal to the prophets,
    and he would reveal another who would surpass him.
    He is the Lord of the prophets. His servants proclaim [this] about him.

13 Hope came to the people. [But] the people gave up its hope
    and sent it to the house of the peoples, and they were without hope.
    The peoples hastened to clothe themselves with the hope that [the people] had sent out.

14 The prophets waited for hope so that they might see.
    Who would not be surprised that the madmen, upon seeing him,
    hastened to insult him, [asking] why he had come in their days?

15 For this is the reason that he had come in their days:
    that if they received him, they might live, and that if they rejected him,
    they would know how insane they were to reject their light.

16 It is difficult for the unjust one to know that he is unjust
    because he does not perceive his wickedness as long as he does not suffer injustice.
    He will learn, through his suffering, the meaning of his wickedness.

The End [of the first two hymns]

---

[40] Mk 8:28
[41] Jn 10:20

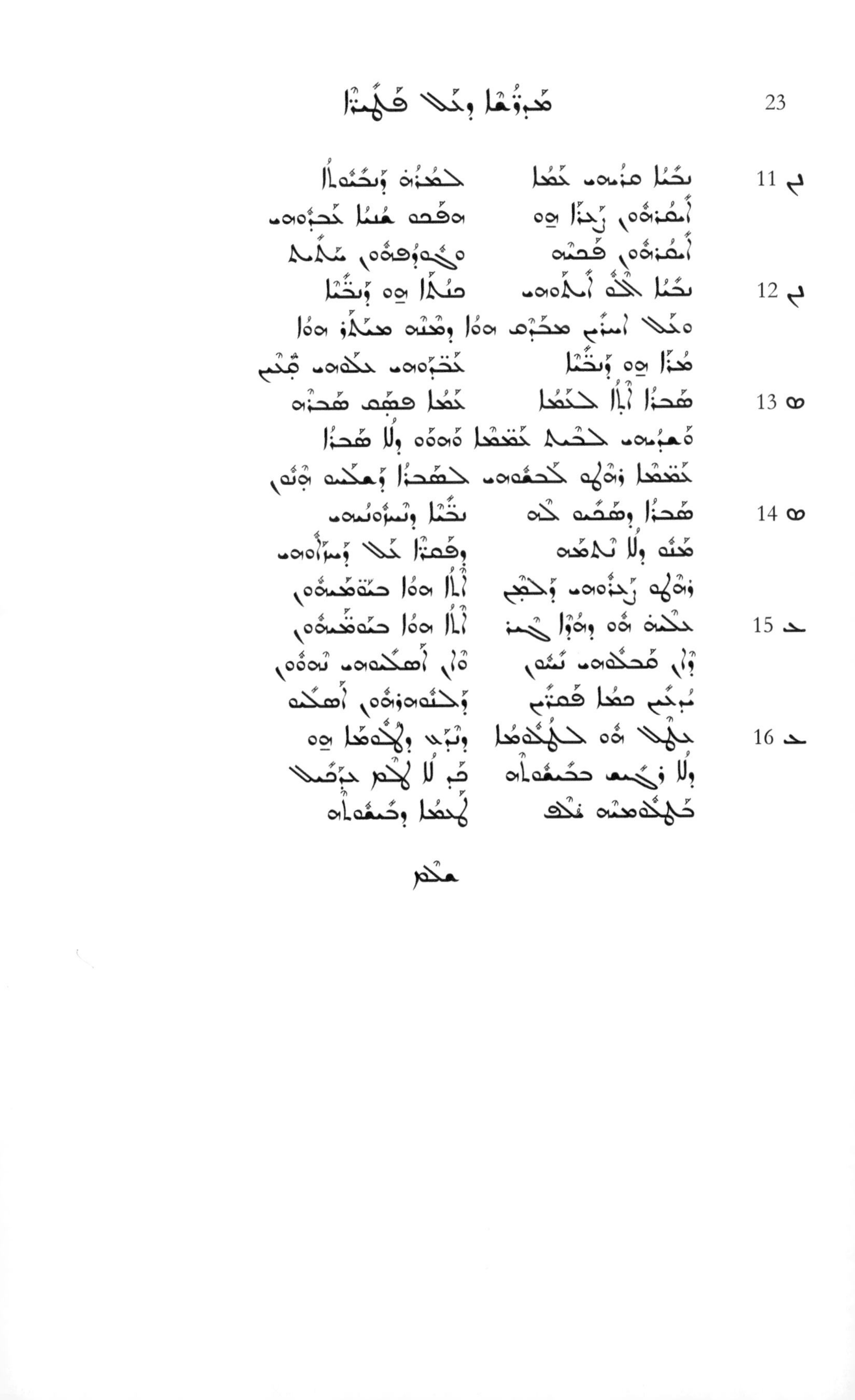

Hymn 3[42]

Again on the unleavened bread, to the tune of
"Gather together to celebrate in the month of Nisan"

1. Behold! The paschal lamb was slain in Egypt,
   and the true lamb was slaughtered in Zion.

   *Response: Praise be to the son, the lord of symbols
   who, through his crucifixion, fulfilled all symbols!*

2. Let us consider both lambs, my brothers and sisters,
   let us see whether they are the same or different.

3. Let us weigh and compare the achievements
   of the symbolic lamb and the true lamb.

4. Let us see the symbolic [lamb] as a shadow,
   let us see the true [lamb] as the fulfillment.

5. Listen to the common symbols of that Passover
   and the double victory of our Passover.

6. There was from Egypt, through the paschal lamb,
   an exodus for the people and not an entry.

7. And there was from Error, through the true lamb,
   an exodus for the peoples and not an entry.

8. And [there was] from Sheol, through the living lamb,
   an exodus for the dead like [the exodus] from Egypt.

9. In Egypt was shown a pair of symbols:
   for Sheol and for Error, [Egypt] was a mirror.

---

[42] For another English translation and analysis of this hymn, see S.P. Brock, "The Poetic Artistry of St. Ephrem," *Parole de l'Orient* 6-7 (1975-76): 21-28.

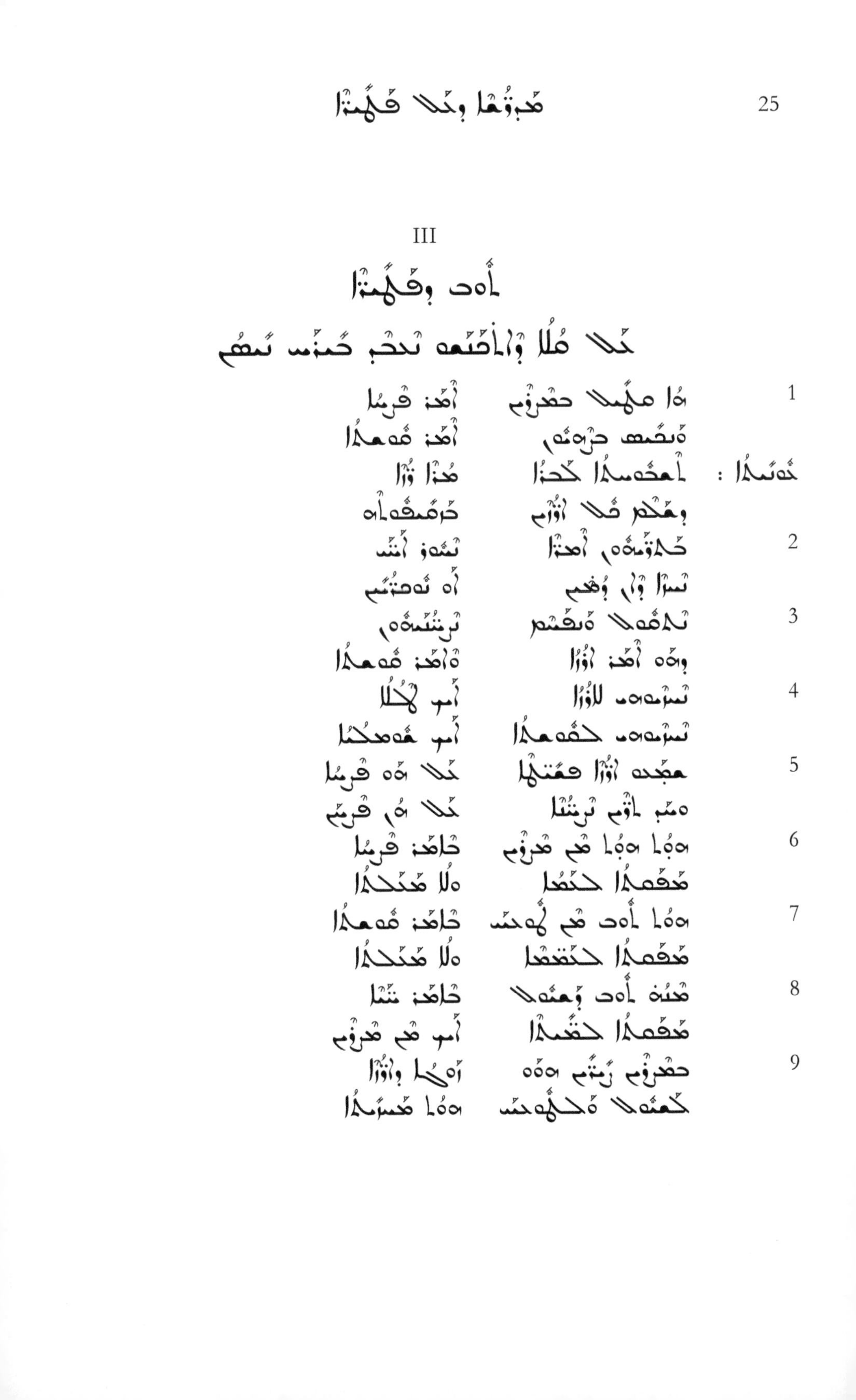

III

10 The greed of Egypt, through the paschal lamb,
    learned to give back, which was not its custom.

11 The hunger of Sheol, through the lamb of life,
    vomited and gave back, which was not its nature.

12 The voracious Error, through the true lamb,
    vomited, spat out, and sent out the peoples who received life.

13 As a result of that paschal lamb, Pharaoh sent out
    the people whom, as though they were dead, he had detained.

14 As a result of the living lamb, death sent out
    the righteous who came forth from their graves.[43]

15 As a result of the true lamb, Satan gave back
    the peoples whom, like Pharaoh, he had detained.

16 In Pharaoh was shown a pair of types:
    for death and for Satan, he was an example.

17 Egypt was opened by the paschal lamb,
    and before the Hebrews, it straightened a path [for exit].

18 Through that true lamb, the true road
    was opened by Satan, who blocked roads.

19 The lamb of life prepared for those entombed
    a road from the grave with a loud cry.[44]

---

[43] Matt 27:52
[44] Mk 15:37

10		
11		
12		
13		
14		
15		
16		
17		
18		
19		

Hymn 4

To the same tune

1 Hear about the type that was revealed in Egypt,
hear about what is revealed and hidden in Zion.

*Response: Praise to the son who through his resurrection
has perfected all the types that his servants have drawn!*

2 Our Lord humiliated Sheol and Error;
he utterly defeated Death and Satan.[45]

3 For our Lord split apart Error, which was in Sheol
in order to teach what is hidden through what is revealed.

4 Just as he split Sheol by revealed things,
so also did he split Error by hidden things.

5 Just as he defeated visible Death,
so also did he defeat Satan invisibly.

6 Many saw that the graves were split,
but they did not see that Satan was defeated.

7 Through what is near, he gave a demonstration
of what was hidden and far away.

8 For although Death will be defeated in the end,
on that Friday,[46] [Death] killed the one who gives life to all.

9 When the people repented, Satan was ashamed;
but on that Friday, he strangled the one who conquers all.

---

[45] In this hymn, Sheol, Error, and Death are personified characters.
[46] Lit: "day of preparation;" Jn 19:14.

IV
	1
		2
	3
		4
		5
		6
		7
		8
		9

10 Egypt was frightened by the paschal lamb;
    the lamb who was killed [also] killed [Egypt's] firstborn.

11 Error was frightened because it saw
    the lamb of truth that exposed his deceits.

12 Sheol also heard [the lamb], and [Sheol's] heart burst
    because of the living voice that gave life to her dead.

13 The paschal lamb only defeated Egypt;
    the true lamb defeated Error and Sheol.

14 In visible Sheol, he split apart Error
    so that they blamed each other that they had been defeated.

15 Because of the paschal lamb, Pharaoh lamented;
    he mourned over his first born, the first of his children.

16 Because of the true lamb, the evil one lamented
    that Adam was made righteous, the first of the sinners.

17 Because of the living lamb, death lamented
    that Abel was raised, the original firstborn.

18 [The Lamb] conquered Satan through visible Death
    so that they[47] proclaimed to one another that the one [lamb] had defeated them.

19 Behold the simple powers in the typological lamb
    and the double victory of the true lamb!

20 Thus the people was ashamed because it was not convinced
    [by] the many mediators who had stood in its midst.

---

[47] Satan and Death

10		
11		
12		
13		
14		
15		
16		
17		
18		
19		
20		

21 For [the people] was not convinced [by] its own paschal symbols,
which are engraved and stamped on our paschal lamb.

22 Even the teachers were ashamed that they alienated the Son,
for behold, they neglected the Law and all its imprints.

23 Behold, the prophets bore, like servants,
examples of the Messiah who rules over all.

24 Nature and Scripture bore together
symbols of his humanity and his divinity.

25 Thus were the people ashamed! For their covenants
were made into a mirror for our covenants.

26 But to you be worship, O Lord of our passover,
because the passover in Egypt declared your symbol.

27 Again to you be praise, O Lord of the prophets,
because all of your prophets declared your types.

28 To you be thanks, O Lord of nature,
because all of nature worships you completely.

Hymn 5

To the same tune

1 The lamb of God led, by his blood,
the peoples from Error as [he led the people] from Egypt.

*Response: Praise to the son who redeemed us by his blood
just as his symbol redeemed the children of Jacob!*

2 Many lambs were slain,
and by that one alone was Egypt defeated.

	21
	22
	23
	24
	25
	26
	27
	28

V

	1
		:
	2

3   Lambs were offered on feast days,
    and by that one alone was Error defeated.

4   Samuel offered a suckling lamb,[48]
    and by it the mighty men and force of the Philistines were defeated.

5   Humbled by the lamb—the son of David,
    was the mighty evil one—the invisible Goliath.

6   The priests took the veil from the holy place,[49]
    and with pure purple they dressed him.

7   Just as they slandered him with [the accusation] of the head-tax:[50]
    "He is the one who prevents people from giving,"[51]

8   so also did they slander him with the garment
    of purple [they put] on him, crying out against him.

9   They feared that he might not die
    so they cast purple upon him in order to kill him.

10 They gave purples [to] kings of the earth—
    to the Maccabees[52] and to Simon, the high priest.[53]

---

[48] 1 Sam 7:9

[49] This is a reference to the "veil over the altar" that was supposed to be a purple cloth according to Num 4:13. See also HCrux 4.3. This was likely the result of the fact that the Old Syriac (S) text of Matt 28:28 states that the soldiers mocked Jesus by clothing him in a purple cloak. Later versions of the Syriac NT, including the Peshitta, omit this word, see G.A. Kiraz, ed., *Comparative Edition of the Syriac Gospels: Aligning the Sinaiticus, Curetonianus, Peshitta, and Harklean Versions, Vol. 1: Matthew*, 3rd ed. (Piscataway, NJ: 2004), 434. Cf. Beck, *Paschahymnen* (Translation), 9, note 4; Rouwhorst, *Les hymnes pascales*, II, 16, note 2.

[50] Matt 22:17; Mk 12:14; Lk 20:22

[51] Lk 23:2

[52] 1 Macc 10:62

[53] 1 Macc 14:43

3		
4		
5		
6		
7		
8		
9		
10		

11 They took some of [the purple] and cast it upon the son of the king,
    and they prophesied about him, like Caiphas [had prophesied].[54]

12 They cast royalty upon the son of David;
    they made him king, even though they did not want to.

13 Wanting to snatch from him what was already his,
    they [unintentionally] gave him another kingdom.

14 For he is the King of Kings, the giver of diadems;
    the whole kingdom is united before him.

15 In that[55] feast was sprinkled
    the blood of the paschal lamb upon all the doors.

16 In this feast is mixed
    the blood of the true lamb among the generations.

17 In that feast the provisional lamb
    gave to that people provisional salvation.

18 In this feast, Error fled
    because of the true lamb who taught the truth.

19 That lamb of symbols was replaced
    by the fulfillment that came and completed the symbols.

20 The truth of the lamb of truth will not come to an end.
    Who will be great enough to replace him?

21 For what lamb will be able to dismiss
    the lamb of God, who dismisses the symbols?

---

[54] Jn 11:51

[55] Even though Ephrem uses the near demonstrative pronoun throughout the following comparisons of the Jewish and Christian paschal feasts, I have used the English demonstratives "this" and "that" in order to bring out the way he is distinguishing between them.

11		
12		
13		
14		
15		
16		
17		
18		
19		
20		
21		

22 The fulfillment came [and] he dressed [himself]
    in the symbols that the Holy Spirit had woven for him.

23 The symbol [was] in Egypt; the truth [is] in the Church;
    the seal of reward [is] in the kingdom.

Hymn 6

To the same tune

1   Between lamb and lamb stand the disciples;
    they ate the paschal lamb and the true lamb.

    Response: To you be praise, King Christ,
    because through your blood your holy church was delivered!

2   The apostles stand in the middle between symbol and reality;
    they saw that the symbol had passed and reality had arrived.

3   Blessed are they, [for in them] was the fulfillment
    of the symbol and the beginning of reality.

4   Our Lord ate the passover with his disciples;[56]
    through the bread that he broke, he abolished the unleavened bread.

5   The bread that gives life to all gave life to the peoples,
    as opposed to the unleavened bread, for those who ate it died.

6   The Church gave us the living bread
    instead of the unleavened bread that Egypt gave.

7   Mary gave us the bread of rest
    instead of the bread of fatigue that Eve gave.

---

[56] Lk 22:7-20

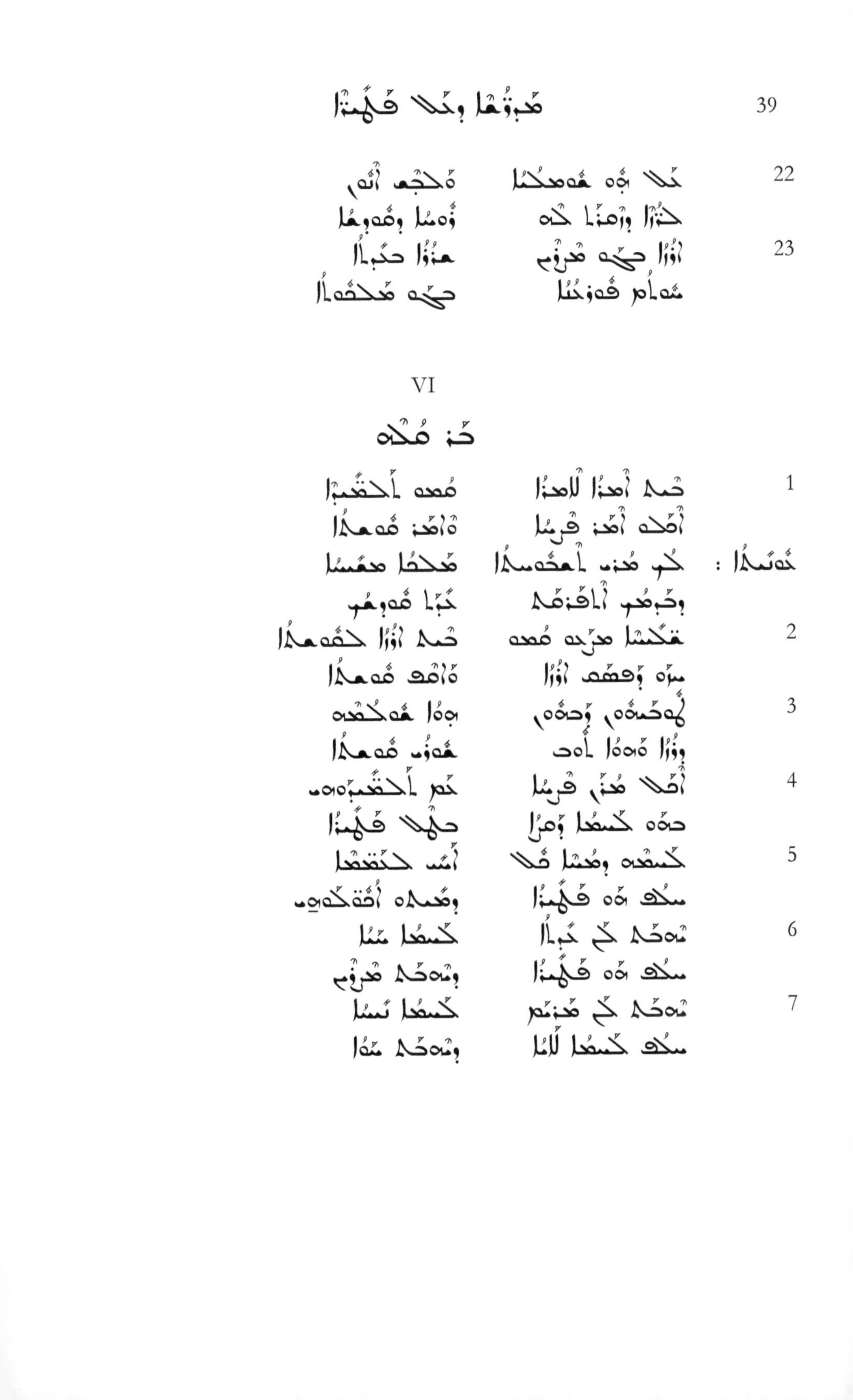

VI

8   Abel was a lamb and he offered a lamb;[57]
    who has seen a lamb offer another lamb?

9   The lamb of God ate a lamb;
    who has seen a lamb eat another lamb?

10 The true lamb ate the paschal lamb;
    the symbol hastened to enter the belly of truth.

11 For all the types in the holy of holies
    dwelt and anticipated the one who fulfills all.

12 And when the symbols saw the true lamb,
    they tore the curtain[58] and stepped out to meet him.

13 They were all entirely based on, and established for, him;
    for they all proclaimed everything [about him] everywhere.

14 For in him, the symbols and types were fulfilled,
    just as he confirmed: "Behold, everything is finished!"[59]

Hymns 7-11 are missing, except for two incomplete hymns that Beck designates as 8 and 9.[60]

[*Hymn 8?*]

[To the same tune]

1   - - - - - -
    They repaid the debt in full.

---

[57] Gen 4:4-8
[58] Matt 27:51
[59] Jn 19:30
[60] For more on the manuscripts, see Beck, *Paschahymnen* (Text), i-iii; Cassingena-Trévedy, *Hymnes Pascales*, 8-11; and Rouwhorst, *Hymnes Pascales*, I, 23-26.

8		
9		
10		
11		
12		
13		
14		

VII – XI desunt

[VIII ?]

1	- - - - - -

2   In that feast, the sea became
    the just avenger for the people treated unjustly.

3   For the sea avenged Joseph:
    it drowned the Egyptians who denied what was owed to him.[61]

4   In the month of flowers,[62] the sea became
    a trap and a refuge, for it saved and killed.

5   In that feast, the flock emerged
    from the depths of the sea, and the wolves drowned.

6   In this feast, the wolves rushed upon
    the shepherd of all, who had become a sheep.[63]

7   In that feast, Moses sang
    a new song of praise over the sea.[64]

8   Between sea and dry land, Moses sang
    of those drowned in the sea and those saved on dry land.

9   Moses, who became radiant,[65] triumphed through the blood[66]
    and acted as God;[67] he achieved [all of this] with a staff.[68]

10 Moses, the pride of the children of the people,
    conquered through the symbols of the son.

---

[61] This could also be translated "the Egyptians, who reneged on their deal with him," referring to the land in Goshen promised to Joseph (Gen 47:6) which had (presumably) been taken by the Pharaoh who "did not know Joseph" and began oppressing the Israelites (Ex 1:8-14).

[62] That is, in Nisan, the month in the spring when flowers begin to bloom.

[63] Ephrem abruptly switches from the Passover in Egypt to the death of Christ.

[64] Ex 15:1-18

[65] Ex 34:29

[66] Ex 7:20-25

[67] Ex 4:16

[68] Ex 14:16

2		
3		
4		
5		
6		
7		
8		
9		
10		

11 The object,⁶⁹ as a servant and companion to Moses,
    submitted to him through the symbols of power.

12 The sea, as a servant to Moses—who was also a servant—
    submitted [to him] through the staff of the son of the king.

13 The created, subjected object
    obeyed its companions through the symbol of divinity.

14 So also does humanity obey the one who acquires
    the power of kingship.

15 Thus, his nature also teaches us
    that power accompanies the sign of kingship.

16 In the month of flowers, the Jordan River
    split apart its waves in the presence of the symbol of its Lord.⁷⁰

17 In the time of flowers, voices cried out,
    and the walls [of Jericho] fell in the presence of Joshua.⁷¹

[*Hymn 9?*]

To the same tune

1   In the month of flowers, the sounds
    of Miriam's tambourine rang out in the presence of the people.⁷²

*Response: Praise be to the firstborn who, through his crucifixion,
turned all the peoples toward the one who sent him!*

---

⁶⁹ I.e. the staff.

⁷⁰ Ephrem now shifts to the parting of the Jordan and the defeat of the city of Jericho when the people entered the promised land; Jos 3:14-17; 6:1-25.

⁷¹ Given the parallelism with the previous strophe and the fact that the Syriac names for Joseph and Jesus are the same, the Syriac audience would catch the double entendre that the walls of Jericho fell in the physical presence of Joseph, but through the symbolic presence of Jesus.

⁷² Ex 15:20-21

11		
12		
13		
14		
15		
16		
17		

[IX]
1		
:		

2   The sea roared against the Egyptians;
    the tambourine made the children of Jacob rejoice.

    3-5: Text is too lacunous to translate[73]

6   In Nisan, Hebrew women carried
    their children openly on the sea bed.

7   Fear passed away from the children
    when they saw that the Egyptians[74] had drowned.

8   The children had been hidden in the inner chamber,
    just as Moses was hidden when he was an infant.[75]

9   In Nisan, hidden flowers sprang forth,
    and children came forth from the inner chambers.

10 In that feast, infants and flowers
    rejoiced together in their beautiful Lord.

11 The wombs of the lilies carried flowers,
    and the wombs of the women carried children.

12 They were afraid to cry while enslaved in Egypt;
    their voices, along with their stature, were cast down.

13 In Nisan, the eloquent one brought forth voices
    so that they were not afraid like children.

---

[73] Though Rouwhorst provides a translation of strophes 4-5 based on a reconstruction from a Syriac breviary. Rouwhorst, *Les hymnes pascales II*, 21, note 2.

[74] Literally: "when they watched the ones who drowned drown."

[75] Ex 2:2

2		
3		]
	- - - - -	
	- - -	- - - -
4	[	- - - -
	- -	- -
5	[	-
	- - - - -	- -
6		
7		
8		
9		
10		
11		
12		
13		
	-	

14-15 [Text is too lacunous to translate]

16 - - - - - ... fear in the wilderness;
    the baby chicks can [now] sing because the eagles have perished.

17 The child, who loves to play outside,
    was downcast and hidden away from the killers.

18 Through that paschal lamb, the children could come out;
    like lambs who had been held in seclusion, they leapt out in freedom.

19 The captive lamb that Moses took captive[76]
    saved the captive lambs that had been taken captive.

20 For Moses himself was a captive infant,
    [and] he became the savior of captive infants.

21 Through both the lamb and Moses—both of whom had been
    captive— the flock and its children came to the goal.[77]

22 A pair of captives demonstrated the symbol
    of the captive lamb that saved the peoples.

23 Out of captivity they led the paschal lamb [for the slaughter];
    out of captivity they led the true lamb [for the slaughter].

24 The typological lamb was without blemish,[78]
    and the true lamb was without stain.[79]

25 The sprinkling [of the blood] of the pure one sanctified the people;
    the sprinkling [of the blood] of the innocent one cleansed the peoples.

---

[76] Ex 12:6
[77] I.e. the promised land
[78] Ex 12:5
[79] 1 Pet 1:19

14	- -	- -
	- -	- -
15	- - - - -	- -
	- -	- - - -
16	- - - - -	
17		
18		
19		
20		
21		
22		
23		
24		
25		
		]

49

Hymn 12

[To the same tune]...[80]

1. In this feast is repaid
   the debt of all by the Lord of all.[81]

2. In this feast our Lord poured out
   the treasures which were filled with the symbols of his death.

3. In this feast our Lord dismissed the symbols
   that struggled in his proclamation.

4. In this feast the lamb of truth abolished
   the paschal lamb, which had run its course.

5. Our Lord ate the passover and broke his body;
   <u>the eater himself became what is eaten.</u>

6. This feast is the invisible furnace
   that reveals the impurity[82] of Iscariot.

7. This is the feast that expelled [Judas] and sent him away
   from the house of truth as a false one.

8. In this feast was purchased
   the Lord of everything for nothing.

9. In this feast the thief sold
   the liberator of all as a slave.

---

[80] Opening lines are missing, as evidenced by the lack of a heading and "response" in the manuscripts.

[81] The word *gawa* generally means "common" or "communal," but neither of these words serves the purpose here of denoting the universality of the debt owed by all humans and the lordship of Christ over all humanity, hence the non-literal translation "debt/Lord" of all."

[82] As in, the impurities that are purged from precious metals when heated in a furnace.

XII

....

1		
2		
3		
4		
5		
6		
7		
8		
9		

10 In this feast the false one kissed
    the true mouth that taught the truth.

11 In this feast he was struck on the cheek,
    he who brought forth water from a jawbone.[83]

12 In this feast, he stood in the house of judgment—
    the firstborn who justifies all—in order to be sentenced.

Hymn 13

To the same tune

1 Come, my brothers and sisters, let us celebrate in the month of Nisan
   the feast of the victories of the true lamb!

*Response: Our congregation gives thanks to the paschal lamb
who slaughtered the ravenous wolves in Nisan!*

2 He was tied up in the house of Annas,[84] yet hidden within him
   was the power that settled in the midst of the oven.[85]

3 He was silent in the house of the judge, yet hidden within him
   were the mouths of wisdom that conquer all.

4 He silenced the thunder of his voice within himself,
   which had frightened the people at Mt. Sinai.[86]

5 They bound and led him, yet silent within him
   was the power that binds all creatures.

---

[83] Judg 15:19
[84] John 18:30
[85] Dan 3:8-30
[86] Exod 20:18

		10
		11
		12

XIII

		1
		:
		2
		3
		4
		5

6   Judas kissed him, yet silent within him
    was the imposition of silence he gave to the demon that cried out.[87]

7   Herod questioned him and mocked him,[88] and he was silent,
    yet all tongues resided within him.

8   He rode upon the cross, even though secretly
    he rode upon the chariot of the Cherubim.[89]

9   They gave him bitter gall,[90] yet hidden within him
    was the sweetness that could make bitterness sweet.[91]

10 He thirsted and asked for water,[92] yet hidden within him
    was the source of water that gave life to all.

11 Pilate washed and cleansed his hands[93]
    in order to condemn the people that stained its hands.

12 The clay [formed] from his spit gave sight to a blind man[94]
    in order to accuse the people: "Why is he disgraced?"

13 The Lord of all received the spit
    from the splendor of a Seraph [which] cannot be depleted.

14 The Cherubim and Seraphim, while he was disgraced,
    hid their faces because they feared the sight.

15 While he was mocked, Michael trembled;
    shocked, amazed and astonished also was Gabriel.

---

[87] Lk 4:41
[88] Lk 23:11
[89] See the vision of the Chariot in Ezekiel 1.
[90] Matt 27:48
[91] Ex 15:23-25
[92] Jn 19:28
[93] Matt 27:24
[94] Jn 9:6

6		
7		
8		
9		
10		
11		
12		
13		
14		
15		

16 Because there was no veil for creation,
    so that it might cover its face as with a garment,

17 darkness spread so that, like Shem and Japheth,[95]
    it would not see the shame of its pure Lord.

18 But when he cried out, the wind[96]
    greatly magnified his cry against the Temple.

19 When she[97] heard that he lowered his head and cried out,[98]
    she tore the curtain as though terrified.

20 Creation wrapped itself in mourning cloaks
    and shrouded itself with darkness because of [the death of] the Son of the Lord.

21 The glorious presence of the Temple, as if it were her garment,
    tore the curtain [in mourning] because of her beloved.

22 Creation asked for a mourning cloak,
    spread it over everything, and bowed her head

23 in order to shame the daughter of Zion, whose head was uncovered
    and [whose] hands were stained by the all sufficient blood.

24 The heavens that illuminated when he was baptized
    grew darker and darker while he suffered.

25 He hid his glory within himself [so that]
    shame was able to approach the all glorious one.

26 The Red Sea dried up immediately because it saw him;
    how could the spit even touch his face?

---

[95] Gen 9:23
[96] This should be read as a double entendre of spirit/wind.
[97] Referring back to the spirit/wind of the previous strophe.
[98] Jn 19:30

16		
17		
18		
19		
20		
21		
22		
23		
24		
25		
26		

27   He stood within the court, yet hidden within him
was the great court that is to come.

28   He was given a crown of thorns among the crucifiers,[99]
he who will come in glory with the angels.

29   He was given a crown of thorns, yet hidden within him
was the power to construct and destroy all.

30   He was placed in a tomb [of rocks], yet silent within him
was the voice that splits hard rocks.

31   He was embalmed and buried, yet hidden within him
was the power that had given life to the bones in the valley.[100]

32   He was bound as a corpse,[101] yet bound [within him] was the voice
that had called Lazarus,[102] who was [also] bound.

Hymn 14

Again to the same tune

1   During a meal, a woman kissed his feet,[103]
and yet, he is the Lord of chastity.

*Response: Praise to the Messiah who came to die
so that through his death the children of Adam might live!*

2   The sinful woman approached the one who atones all,
whose mouth was the hyssop that washes away sins.

---

[99] Mk 15:17
[100] Ezek 37:1-14
[101] As in: wrapped in burial cloths.
[102] Jn 11:43
[103] Lk 7:38

	27
	28
	29
	30
	31
	32

XIV

	1
	:
	2

3   The reproachful ones reproached him [saying], "He does not know,"[104] yet all knowledge was hidden within him.

4   Mary[105] anointed him there, yet a Cherub
    is not even permitted to approach his head.

5   She leaned upon his breast, like John,[106]
    so that he might honor the lowly before the high.

6   Thus, he demonstrated that he had loved Adam
    when he was chaste and holy, like John.

7   Thus, he demonstrated that, like John,
    the holy virgins are also beloved.

8   For in the one whom he loved, he gave a pledge
    that he would love all the chaste ones.

9   Iscariot became angry with the blessed woman;[107]
    in the guise of representing the poor, the thief judged [her].

10 Our lord heard [this] and refrained from exposing it,
    yet he is the furnace for all accusations.[108]

11 The mystery that he kept secret from the disciples
    he revealed to John as a friend.

12 Virginity approached near the chaste one;
    he demonstrated that the daughter of his symbol is chastity.

---

[104] Lk. 7:39
[105] Jn 12:3
[106] Jn 13:24-25
[107] Jn 12:4-6
[108] That is, the "testing fire;" cf. Hymn 12.6 above.

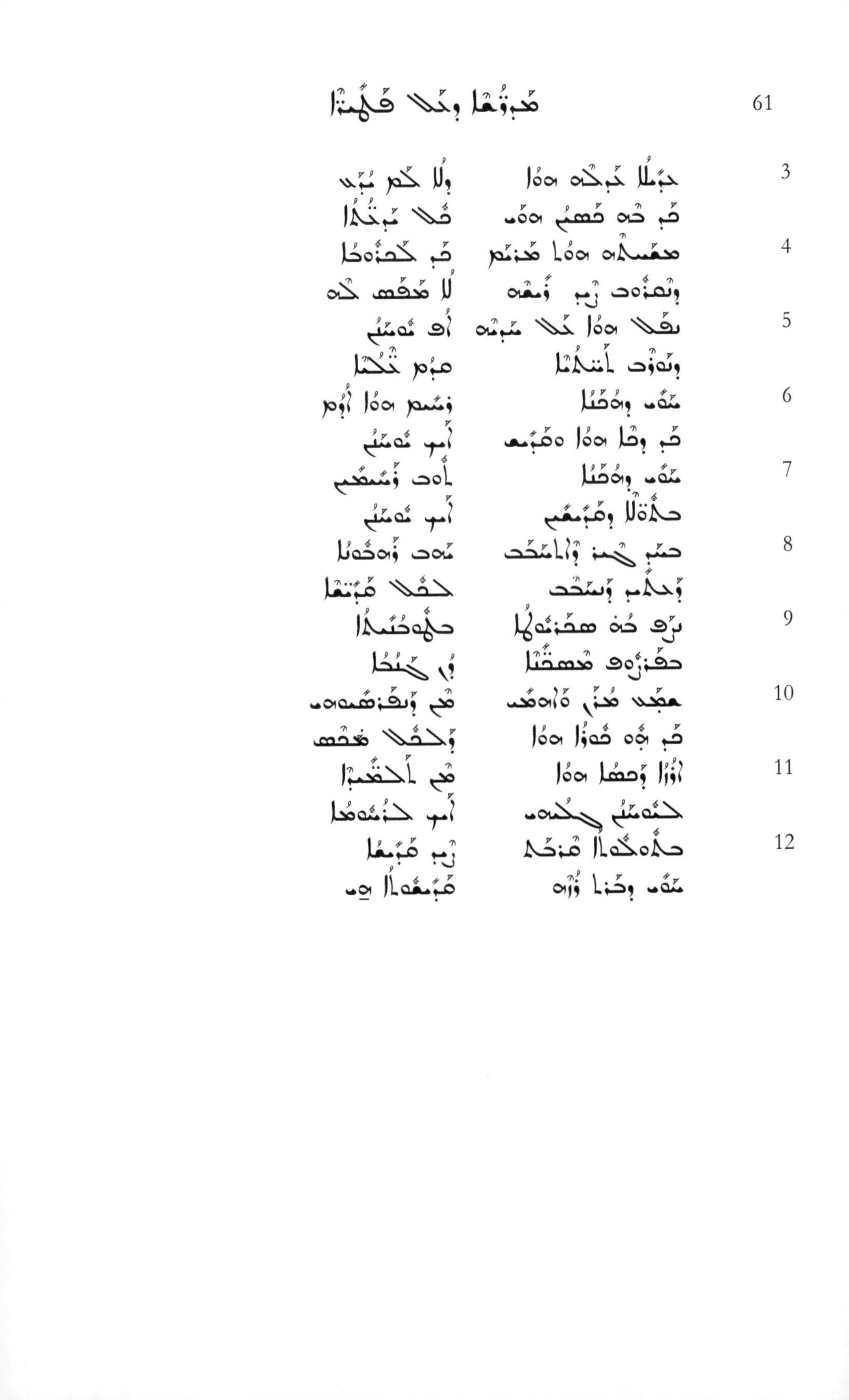

13 He dipped the bread and gave it to the thief,[109]
    and he revealed himself even though [Jesus] did not force him[110]

14 For he waited patiently, that sweet one,
    for that scoundrel to accuse himself.

15 He dipped the bread and gave to him hidden death;
    the medicine of life had been washed from the bread.

16 The one who gives life to all blessed the food,
    [and] it became the medicine of life for those who ate it.

17 Thus, the bread that had been washed of the blessings
    was taken by the cursed one, the second snake.

18 He took the bread and separated [himself] from the disciples;
    he separated himself, even though no one pushed him away.

19 Our Lord did not separate him [from the group] so that no one could blaspheme
    [by claiming] that coercion, rather than [free] will, had forced [Judas].

20 Although he did not incite [Judas], our Lord did draw him out;
    but when he separated [himself] and departed, he did not push him away.

21 It was a good thing that [Jesus] had chosen [Judas]
    it was a bad thing that [Judas] rejected himself.

22 But when the hidden wolf separated [himself] and departed
    from among the flock of the twelve,

23 the true lamb stood up and broke his body
    for the sheep who had eaten the paschal lamb.

---

[109] Jn 13:26
[110] Jn 13:21-30

13		
14		
15		
16		
17		
18		
19		
20		
21		
22		
23		

24 Thus he completed the type that had hastened
    from the midst of Egypt until that time.

Hymn 15

To the same tune

1   When God descended upon Mt. Sinai,
    it was by [God's] power that the mountain could bear him.

    *Response: Praise be to the son who through his blood saved us
    like his symbol saved the children of Jacob!*

2   The mountain melted away before him,[111]
    [but] the power of its creator sustained it.

3   For only through the power of the creator
    are the created things able to serve.

4   Through his power, the heavens lift up his glory
    Thus it is that he supports them, and they bear him.

5   He gave power also to the Cherubim,
    [and] the chariot carries him only because he gives it power.

6   He also lived in the Temple because his loving mercies desired
    that he should be made known there for whoever sought him.

7   For, in order that whoever seeks him might not wander,
    he dwelt in the Temple, even though he is everywhere.

8   The cloud that dwelt in [the temple] received from him
    the power through which it was able to become his bridal chamber.

---

[111] Ps. 97:5

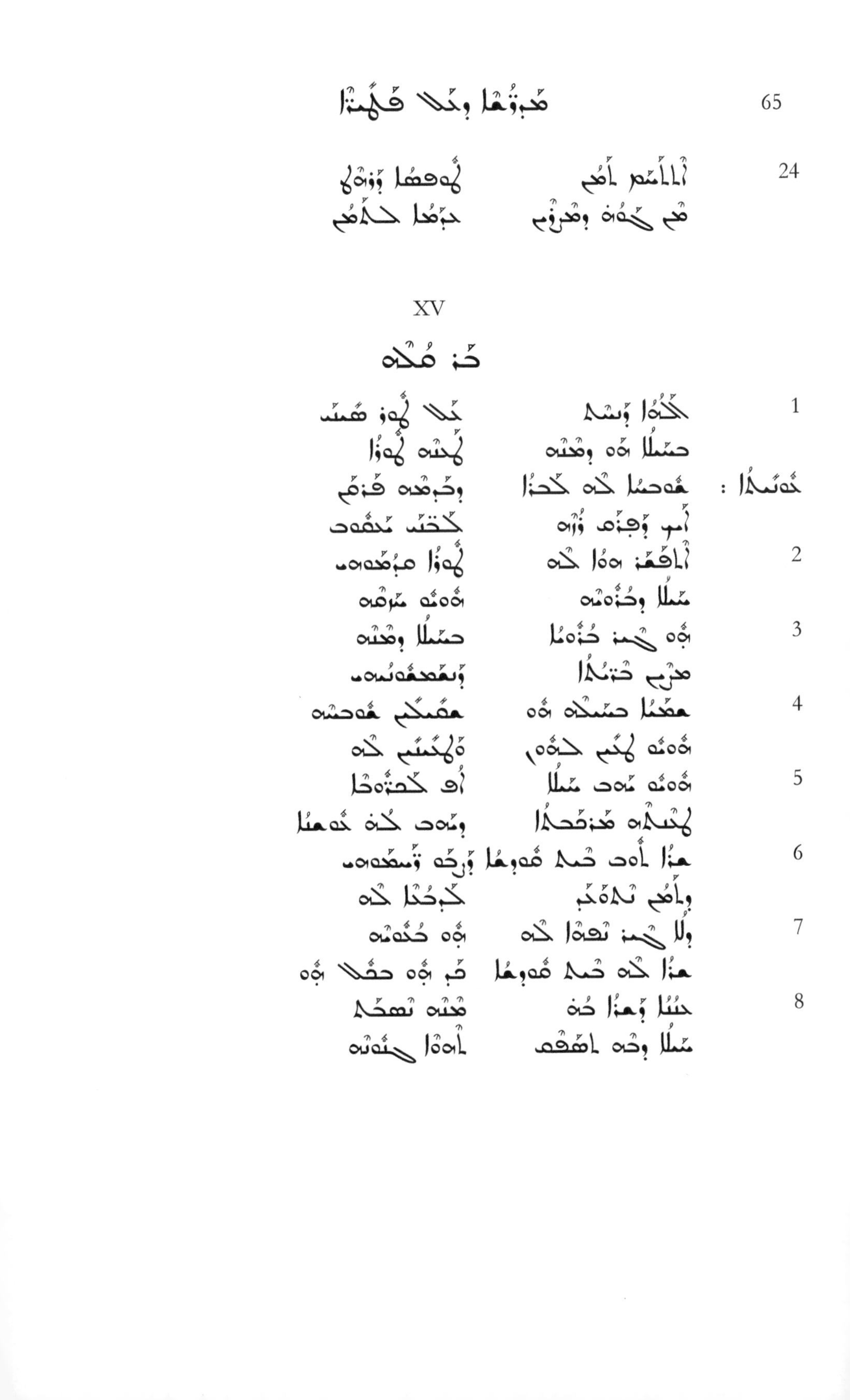

XV

9   The apostles—mere fishermen—with his colors
    were able to fashion prototypes of his symbols.

10 The prophets, as painters, painted him
    because he taught them whom he resembled.

11 With his colors, they were able to paint his beauty;
    they saw how much he resembles the Father.

12 Through his power, kings retain
    their position of kingship until he comes.

13 Through his atonement, priests were able
    to atone for sins through the symbol of his sacrifices.

14 Through his power, the sea lifts itself up,
    for it is not able to bear its own weight.

15 For a created thing cannot be equal to the power of the creator;
    for if it could suffice for him, it would be like him.

16 The entire [creation] is not even sufficient for he who is the Lord of
    all; and if it could suffice for him, it would be equal to him.

17 The creation is weak before the creator
    because it is through his power that it obeys him.

18 Before him Mt. Sinai was melted.
    It is a miracle! How did the cross hold him?

19 The mountain of rock is not able to hold him;
    how did a donkey of flesh carry him?[112]

---

[112] Matt 21:6

9		
10		
11		
12		
13		
14		
15		
16		
17		
18		
19		

20 The sun that gives light to all looked at him and darkened;[113]
    how did that people of darkness look upon him?

21 The fever saw him and fled and escaped;[114]
    so how did Zion rage against him?

22 The fig tree saw him and withered immediately,[115]
    yet the hand that struck him did not wither?

23 Demons and pigs fell into the sea;[116]
    how did Caiphas and his comrades crucify him?

24 The mighty Legion howled before him;[117]
    how could the evil servant strike him?[118]

25 The withered hand was stretched out to him by a word[119]
    so that the hand that struck him might be denounced.

26 He gave the haul of fish to Simon as one from above,
    yet he asked and ate from it as a lowly one.[120]

27 He brought Lazarus to life as God,
    yet he asked about his grave as a mere human.[121]

28 He drove out the demons as the one who has mercy on all,
    yet he asked about the child as one who has to learn all.[122]

---

[113] Mk 15:33
[114] Mk 1:31
[115] Mk 11:12-14
[116] Mk 5:13
[117] Mk 5:6-9
[118] Jn 18:22
[119] Mk 3:1-5
[120] Jn 21:1-13
[121] Jn 11:34
[122] Mk 9:21

20		
21		
22		
23		
24		
25		
26		
27		
28		

29 He revealed hidden things to the disciples;
    he asked and learned things about revealed things.

30 He chose Judas as if he did not know,
    yet he gave the "woe" as if he knew everything.[123]

31 Mary poured out oil upon his head;
    the gift that was from him, she returned to him.

Hymn 16

To the same tune

1   The firstborn willed [it] and enclosed the small grave,
    for nothing that he willed could be prevented.

    Response: Praise be to the creator of all who, because of his love for us, submitted his power to the cross!

2   Concerning everything that he wills: it is not possible
    to prevent his will from whatever he wills.

3   For he willed it, and everything came into being,
    [and] because he willed it, created things came to be.

4   He willed it, and he enclosed himself in the belly of hell,
    and because he willed it, he enclosed himself in the womb of Mary.

5   Because he willed it, greedy death devoured him;
    it devoured him, but then spat him back out because he willed it.

6   He hid his life within himself so that
    death, which was dead, was able to devour the living.

7   His life-giving fragrance drifted into Sheol,
    which vomited and threw him out because it could not bear him.

---

[123] Matt 26:24

29		
30		
31		

XVI

1		
:		
2		
3		
4		
5		
6		
7		

8   He willed it, and they took him captive. And his captors
    took him captive because he hid his power within himself.

9   For when he released just a breath of his power,
    all of his captors fell and bowed down.[124]

10 And when they threw him down from the mountain,[125]
    he did not want to be harmed, so he was not harmed.

11 But when they threw him down, he flew[126] and showed them
    how bodies will be carried away in the end.[127]

12 He made the air like a chariot,
    and his body was the driver.

13 For the air will be like a chariot:
    it will fly the righteous up to meet its Lord.

14 A chariot came down for Elijah,
    [and] it flew down without a driver.

15 Fiery horses were harnessed to it;[128]
    they themselves served as the driver.

16 This is also the case with the chariot of the Cherubim
    whose driver is silent [and] invisible.

---

[124] Jn 18:5-6
[125] Lk 4:29
[126] For more on the early Syriac interpretive tradition of Lk 4:29-30 and the "flying Jesus," see T. Baarda, "'The Flying Jesus': Luke 4:29-30 in the Syriac Diatessaron," *Vigiliae Christianae* 40 (1986): 313-341.
[127] Referring to the "rapture," cf. 1 Thess 4:17
[128] 2 Kgs 2:11

8		
9		
10		
11		
12		
13		
14		
15		
16		

17 The silent will of that silent[129] one
   guides the chariot along with creation.

18 For still and silent is that creator of all;
   through his silent will, he guides all.

19 Thunder is born from his stillness
   and great lightening from his silence.

20 Being silent and still, he stirs up creation;
   with one quiet symbol, he fills creation.

21 He willed it and made whatever he willed,
   and he creates again however he wills.

22 It is he that struck the earth with the rod of his mouth;
   with the breath of his lips, he kills the wicked.[130]

23 The wicked Iscariot kissed him
   because he did not want the breath of his mouth to kill him.

24 It is a wonder that the chaff could kiss the fire;[131]
   the fire held its power and did not harm him.

25 [The fire] displayed meakness before him,
   [whereas Judas] made for himself a noose.

26 The hands that took a price for their Lord—
   they also hung [Judas] with a noose.

27 The mouth that kissed the fiery coal[132]
   its lips were cold like [those] of a hanged man.

---

[129] Ephrem employs two different roots for words meaning "silent/silence/stillness" in these strophes.
[130] Isa 11:4
[131] Matt 3:12; Lk 3:17
[132] Isa 6:7

		17
		18
		19
		20
		21
		22
		23
		24
		25
		26
		27

28 Because he dwelt in greed,
    his body burst open from lust.[133]

29 The noose suspended him in the air[134]
    because he betrayed the Messiah who flies in the air.

30 He was suspended between earth and heaven
    because he betrayed the earthly and heavenly one.

31 He betrayed the son, who is heavenly,
    but he killed the body, which is earthly.

32 The sky rejoiced,[135] for he betrayed its lord;
    the earth rejoiced, for he killed its king.

33 Through his own power, the wood [of the cross] held him;
    the wood did not burn [even though] it held the fire.

34 Behold, from what belonged to him, the givers gave;
    behold, from the house of his treasure, the takers took.

35 With the myrrh[136] that he created, Joseph anointed him;
    with what belonged to him, the buriers buried him.

Hymn 17

To the same tune

1 Nisan, [the month] that restores all roots
   was not able to restore that aged people.

   Response: Blessed are you who rejected the people and their unleavened bread because their hands were stained with the precious blood!

---

[133] Act 1:18
[134] Matt 27:5
[135] The earth and sky rejoiced at Judas' death.
[136] Jn 19:39

28		
29		
30		
31		
32		
33		
34		
35		

XVII

1		
:		

2   For when they left [Egypt], the people carried
    the leaven of impiety[137] along with the unleavened bread.

3   For Moses did not allow [the people] in Egypt
    to add leavened bread to the unleavened.[138]

4   In this way, he taught [them] to separate
    the leaven of the Egyptians from their thought.

5   The unleavened bread is a symbol of the living bread;
    the old ones ate the new symbol.

6   Moses revealed the symbol that renews all,
    [and] he gave it to the profligate people who desire flesh.

7   The flesh from the earth weighed them down,
    and their mind lowered to greedy desire.

8   The earthly ones ate the heavenly manna,
    [and] they became dust in the earth through their sins.

9   The spiritual bread flies and makes [everything] light
    so the peoples flew up to dwell in paradise.

10 Through that one who enters [paradise], everyone enters it;
    through Adam, the one who departed [from paradise], all departed.

11 Since the body is there—the second Adam[139]—
    the hungry eagles[140] gathered together before him.

12 Through the spiritual bread everyone becomes
    an eagle that reaches up to paradise.

---

[137] Also: "paganism"
[138] Ex 12:15
[139] 1 Cor 15:47
[140] Matt 24:28; Lk 17:37

2		
3		
4		
5		
6		
7		
8		
9		
10		
11		
12		

13 Whoever eats the living bread of the son
    will also fly to meet him in the clouds.

14 The nature of the unleavened bread is heavy,
    for the symbol is not able to make the people fly.

15 Elijah ate from the pitcher and the jug:[141]
    a small symbol that he flew in the air.

16 It was not a daughter of Jacob that gave the symbol;
    Elijah ate it in the presence of a daughter of the Gentiles.

17 If that symbol of his bread thus caused [Elijah] to fly,
    how much more will it cause the peoples to fly to Eden?

Hymn 18

To the same tune

1 During the Passover, the peoples ate the leavened bread;
   through the ancient food, their mind was renewed.

*Response: Give thanks to the son who gave his body to us
instead of that unleavened that he gave to the people!*

2 Food is not able to renew anyone;
   [only] the heart is able to be renewed.

3 For behold, in Nisan, the bull eats
   the fresh pasture, even while goring.

4 And the people, by eating that unleavened bread,
   stabbed the son with a lance in Nisan.[142]

---

[141] 1 Kgs 17:14-16
[142] Jn 19:34

13		
14		
15		
16		
17		

XVIII

1		
:		
2		
3		
4		

5   Also in fresh pasture, the wild ass becomes fat;
because the people likewise became fat, he kicked them away.[143]

6   If new food can provide benefit [for the eater],
then the beast is better than the people.

7   [The beast] was also better than that [people] because he was reviled by them,
for unlike [the beast, the people] did not know their Lord.[144]

8   The serpent also sheds [its skin] and is renewed;
inasmuch as it sheds the outside, so also it ages on the inside.

9   Behold, the people is renewed outwardly in form
but in their heart dwells deadly bile.

10   For [that people] is like that ancient serpent,
who cunningly gave us the fruit of death.

11   For behold, he gave to us from their unleavened bread
so that it would be in us a deadly poison.

12   Oh people who have aged through the unleavened bread!
Behold! The aged are renewed as through the leavened bread.

13   Oh unleavened bread that gradually
separates the ones who eat it from the pagans!

14   In the new unleavened bread he hid and gave
the ancient leaven of infidelity.

15   It was the symbol of the son [that] Moses hid
within that unleavened bread as the medicine of life.

---

[143] Deut. 32:15
[144] Isa 1:3

		5
		6
		7
		8
		9
		10
		11
		12
		13
		14
		15

16   [Jesus] washed the medicine of life from the unleavened bread
     [and] he gave it to Judas as the poison of death.

17   Thus the deathly poison of Iscariot
     is what one receives from that unleavened bread.

Hymn 19

Again the same tune

1   The true lamb stood up and broke his body
     for the upright ones who had eaten the paschal lamb.

Response: Praise to the messiah who, through his body,
rejected the unleavened bread of the people along with the people!

2   He slaughtered and ate the paschal [lamb], and he broke his body;
     he removed the shadow, and he gave the truth.

3   He ate the unleavened bread, [and] in the unleavened bread,
     his body became for us the true unleavened bread.

4   There the symbol was completed, [the symbol] that had pursued [him]
     from the days of Moses until then.

5   But the evil people who desire our death
     entice us and give to us death in food.

6   Tempting was the tree that Eve saw,
     and likewise, tempting also is the unleavened bread.

7   From that temptation death is revealed;
     in the beautiful unleavened bread death is hidden.

8   Although the dead lion was impure,
     its bitterness gave sweetness.[145]

---

[145] Jud 14:9

16		
17		

XIX

1		
:		
2		
3		
4		
5		
6		
7		
8		

9   In the bitter lion was good honey;
    in the sweet unleavened bread, there is bitter death.

10 The angels were tempted by the unleavened bread
    that Sara had baked[146] because of his symbol [within it].

11 Despise, my brothers and sisters, the unleavened bread
    in which the symbol of Iscariot dwells.

12 Increasingly flee from the unleavened bread, brothers and sisters,
    because stench dwells in its purity.

13 For that word—"rotten"—which Moses wrote,[147]
    behold, it dwells here in the purity of that unleavened bread.

14 Onion and garlic[148] became desirable to the people;
    their unleavened bread stinks, along with their food.

15 From unclean ravens Elijah received bread[149]
    because he knew that they were pure.

16 My brothers and sisters, do not take the unleavened bread
    from the people whose hands are stained with blood,

17 lest [you also take]—stuck to that unleavened bread—
    the filth that fills [the people's] hands.

18 Although the meat is pure, no one eats
    what has been sacrificed because it is stained.

19 Thus how impure is that unleavened bread,
    baked by the hands that killed the son.

---

[146] Gen 18:6
[147] Ex 16:20
[148] Num 11:5
[149] 1 Kgs 17:6

9		
10		
11		
12		
13		
14		
15		
16		
17		
18		
19		

20 The hand that is stained by the blood of animals—
    it is an abomination to take food from it.

21 Therefore, whoever takes from that hand
    is thoroughly stained by the blood of the prophets.

22 My brothers and sisters, let us not eat with the medicine of life
    the unleavened bread of the people as the poison of death.

23 For the blood of the Messiah is mixed and dwells in
    the unleavened bread of the people and in our sacrifice.

24 Whoever partakes in our offering receives the medicine of life;
    whoever eats with the people receives the poison of death.

25 For the blood for which they cried, which will [always] be upon
    them,[150] is mixed in their festivals and in their Sabbaths.

26 And whoever takes part in their festivals
    also comes near the splattering of blood.

27 The people that does not eat from a pig
    is a pig that is splattered with much blood.

28 Flee and remove [yourselves] from [the blood], for behold it is shaken,
    lest you be defiled by the sprinkling of blood.

Hymn 20

To the same tune

1 Come, my brothers and sisters, let us hear about the hidden son
   who revealed his body and hid his power.

---

[150] Matt 27:25

20		
21		
22		
23		
24		
25		
26		
27		
28		

XX

1		

*Response: Praise to the messiah in whom, during this feast,
the cursed people drove nails!*

2   When they nailed his hands, he split open the graves;
    for his will is a free power.

3   They did not bind his power along with his hands;
    his hands were bound, but his power was free.

4   For his body was nailed entirely to the cross,
    but his power was completely and utterly free.

5   His power to overcome was not in his hands,
    [but] in his will that brings about and conquers all things.

6   Even when the hands of our Lord were free,
    it was not with his hands that he bore the dead when he came forth
    [from the dead].

7   It was his hidden power that entered death,
    that carried the bound one,[151] [and] that flew and came forth.

8   Moses also showed through his outstretched hands[152]
    the symbol of [Jesus'] hands: victorious and triumphant.[153]

9   For if it had been the power of his arms,
    how could they conquer from such a distance?

10 For he displayed a hidden power in his arms,
    which dwelt in his arms in order to form symbols.

11 Thus the prophet displayed symbols of the son [with his hands],
    how much more will the firstborn do without his hands?

---

[151] Jn 11:44
[152] Ex 17:11
[153] That is, stretched out to either side, in the fashion of the cross.

:		
2		
3		
4		
5		
6		
7		
8		
9		
10		
11		

12 The will of the son is his treasure from which
    he distributed his wealth wherever he wanted.

13 For his word is the treasure of treasures;
    wherever he opens it, he enriches creation.

14 His gift is the source of good things,
    and when he opens it, he exalts creation.

15 His will is the great key
    by which the treasures of mercies are opened.

16 His goodness is merciful—
    a carrier of medicines like a nurse.

17 Justice is prudent—
    a carrier of threats like a teacher.

18 The hand of his goodness is gentle for all;
    it binds all wounds like a mother.

19 The hand of his justice is difficult for all;
    it cuts all wounds like a doctor.

20 His justice retracted her hand
    when he came to be among humanity.

21 There was no one who spoke against his justice
    except for Satan, as the opposing one.

Hymn 21

To the same tune

1   The Passover meal that was commanded to be pure—
    behold, the one who eats from it is a prostitute.

12		
13		
14		
15		
16		
17		
18		
19		
20		
21		

XXI

1		

Response: Praise be to the one who redeems the peoples through his blood instead of [through] the symbol that redeems only that one people!

2 The feast that was commanded to take place in Zion—[154]
behold, it takes place everywhere as if [that command] were nothing.

3 For Moses did not allow the people
to celebrate its feast wherever they happened to be.

4 For Moses bound the feast to the offering,
and the offering he bound to the Holy of Holies.

5 Thus, that the feast should take place just anywhere
is not allowed because the offering was bound to it,

6 and the offering cannot take place just anywhere
because [Moses] bound it to the holy altar.[155]

7 The feast did not happen without the offering;
the offering was not offered without the Temple.

8 If [Moses] thus, while in the land, did not allow
for the feast to be celebrated outside of Zion,

9 then how can [the people] today, among the Gentiles,
celebrate the feast wherever they want?

10 In Babylon, Daniel did not celebrate the feast;
he dared not celebrate it like the apostates did.

11 Daniel knew that a feast that takes place
where it is not allowed is an impure feast.

---

[154] Deut 16:5-6
[155] Deut 12:2-12

	:	
	2	
	3	
	4	
	5	
	6	
	7	
	8	
	9	
	10	
	11	

12 For in Nisan, the month of feasts,
    Daniel fasted for three weeks.[156]

13 He did not, as he said, eat flesh during his fast;
    thus, he did not eat the paschal lamb.

14 Once a year, Moses celebrated—with sacrifices and drink offerings—
    the consecration of the temporary tabernacle.

15 It was necessary for Moses to sacrifice in the wilderness
    in order to teach the law of sacrifices.

16 He both sacrificed and refrained from sacrifice in order to teach
    that no one should sacrifice wherever he wants.

17 For the people did not sacrifice in the wilderness;
    behold, the prophet proclaimed that they did not sacrifice:

18 "Did you perchance offer me any sacrifices
    or offerings for forty years?"[157]

19 And if anyone breaks this word of truth,
    he is bound to another that Moses spoke:

20 "Let no one behave in that land
    as one does here in the wilderness;"[158]

21 "at the place where your Lord [shall] dwell,
    there will it be permitted for you to offer sacrifice"[159]

22 In Jerusalem alone was it permitted
    to perform the feast and the sacrifices.

---

[156] Dan 10:3
[157] Am 5:25
[158] Deut 12:8
[159] Deut 12:11

12		
13		
14		
15		
16		
17		
18		
19		
20		
21		
22		

23 Through the fig tree our Lord gave a sign
    because it deprived the earth of sacrifices.

24 For instead of the sacrifices of all animals
    that were sacrificed in Jerusalem alone,

25 behold, throughout the whole land,
    the living body, the living sacrifice, is offered today.

The End of the twenty-one hymns concerning the unleavened bread by the Holy St. Ephrem

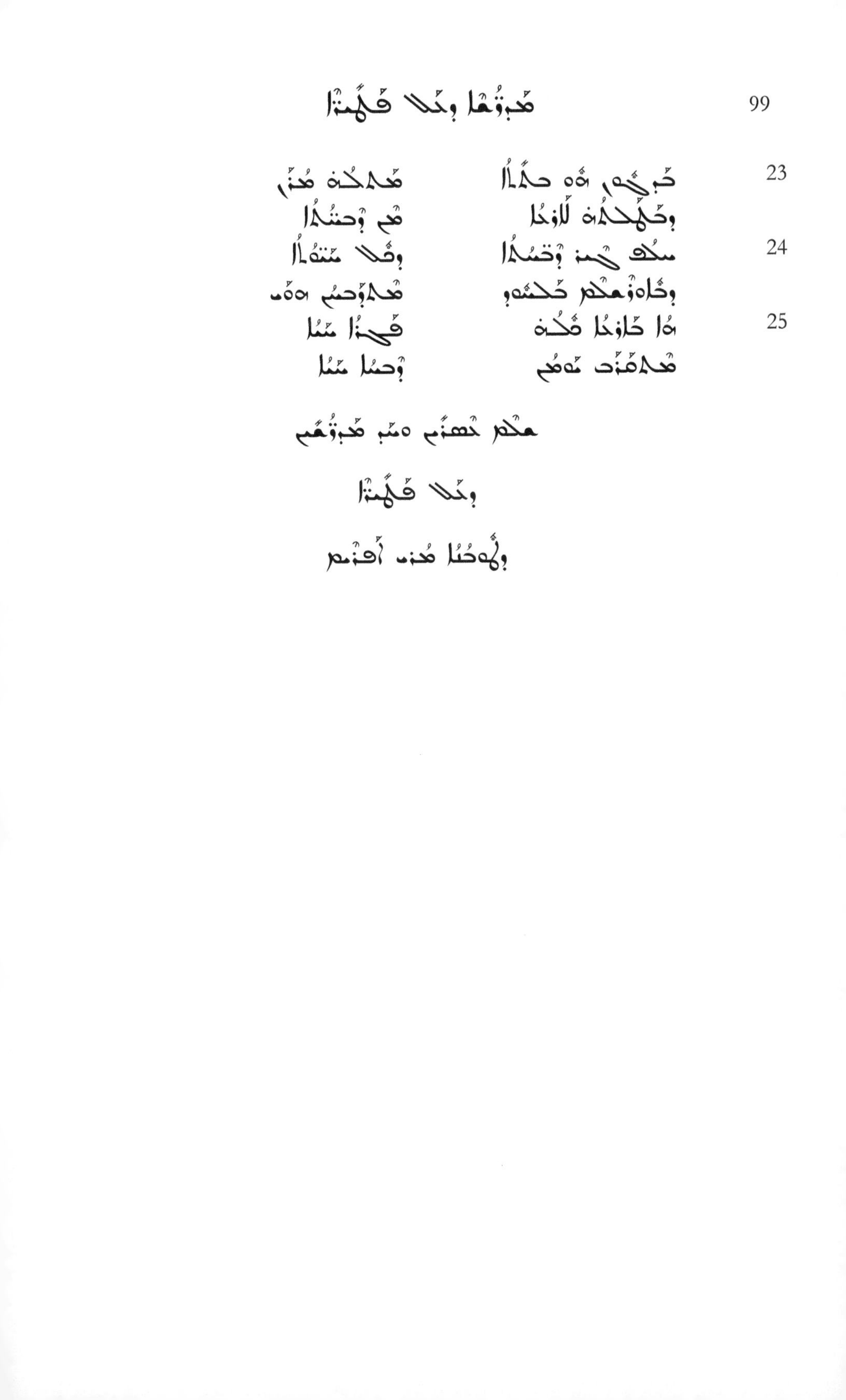

INDEX OF BIBLICAL REFERENCES

Genesis
    4:4-8   40
    9:23   56
    14:18   20
    18:6   86

Exodus
    2:2   46
    4:16   42
    7:20-25   42
    12:5   48
    12:6   48
    12:15   78
    14:16   42
    15:1-18   42
    15:20   44
    15:23-25   54
    16:20   86
    17:11   90
    20:18   52
    34:29   42

Numbers
    4:13   34
    11:5   86

Deuteronomy
    12:2-12   94
    12:8   96
    12:11   96
    16:5-6   94
    32:15   82

Joshua
    3:14-17   44
    6:1-25   44

Judges
    14:9   84
    15:19   52

1 Samuel
    7:9   34

1 Kings
    17:6   86
    17:14-16   80

2 Kings
    2:11   72

Psalms
    97:5   64

Isaiah
    1:3   82
    6:7   74
    11:4   74

Ezekiel
    37:1-14   58

Daniel
    3:8-39   52
    10:3   96

Amos
  5:25   96

1 Maccabees
  10:62   34
  14:43   34

Matthew
  3:12   74
  21:6   66
  22:42   18
  22:17   34
  26:24   68
  27:5   76
  27:24   54
  27:25   88
  27:48   54
  27:51   40
  27:52   26

Mark
  1:31   68
  3:1-5   68
  3:21   20
  5:6-9   68
  5:13   68
  8:28   22
  9:21   68
  10:16   18
  11:12-14 68
  12:14   34
  15:17   58
  15:33   68
  15:37   26
  24:28   78

Luke
  3:17   74
  4:29   72
  4:41   54
  7:38   58
  7:39   60
  17:37   78
  20:22   34
  22:7-20 38
  23:11   54

John
  9:6   54
  10:20   22
  11:34   68
  11:43   58
  11:44   90
  11:51   36
  12:3   60
  12:4-6 60
  13:21-30 62
  13:24-25 60
  13:26   62
  18:5-6 72
  18:22   68
  18:30   52
  19:14   28
  19:28   54
  19:30   40, 56
  19:34   80
  19:39   76
  21:1-13 68

Acts
  1:18   76

1 Corinthians
  1:21   16
  15:47   78

2 Corinthians
8:9 12

1 Peter
1:19 48

Printed in Australia
AUHW011428190721
348889AU00035B/171